# The Latest Ninja Foodi

## Cookbook UK for Beginners

The Surprise Pressure Cook, Dehydrate, Sear/Sauté, Steam, and Slow Cook Recipes for Ninja Foodi MAX Multi-Cooker

Sienna George

# © Copyright 2023 – All Rights Reserved

This document is geared towards providing exact and reliable information with regards to the topic and issue covered. The publication is sold with the idea that the publisher is not required to render accounting, officially permitted, or otherwise, qualified services. If advice is necessary, legal, or professional, a practiced individual in the profession should be ordered. -From a Declaration of Principles which was accepted and approved equally by a Committee of the American Bar Association and a Committee of Publishers and Associations. In no way is it legal to reproduce, duplicate, or transmit any part of this document in either electronic means or in printed format. Recording of this publication is strictly prohibited and any storage of this document is not allowed unless with written permission from the publisher.

All rights reserved. The information provided herein is stated to be truthful and consistent, in that any liability, in terms of inattention or otherwise, by any usage or abuse of any policies, processes, or directions contained within is the solitary and utter responsibility of the recipient reader.

Under no circumstances will any legal responsibility or blame be held against the publisher for any reparation, damages, or monetary loss due to the information herein, either directly or indirectly. Respective authors own all copyrights not held by the publisher.

The information herein is offered for informational purposes solely, and is universal as so. The presentation of the information is without contract or any type of guarantee assurance. The trademarks that are used are without any consent, and the publication of the trademark is without permission or backing by the trademark owner.

All trademarks and brands within this book are for clarifying purposes only and are the owned by the owners themselves, not affiliated with this document.

# Table of Contents

**1** Introduction

**2** Fundamentals of Ninja Foodi Max Multi-Cooker

**15** 4-Week Meal Plan

**17** Chapter 1 Breakfast

| | | | |
|---|---|---|---|
| Taco Huevos Rancheros | 17 | Crescent Rolls | 22 |
| Spanish Tortilla with Sauce | 18 | Almond Cranberry Quinoa | 22 |
| Millet Porridge | 18 | Enchilada Casserole | 23 |
| Spinach Eggs Florentine | 19 | Easy Breads | 23 |
| Lemon-Seasoned Quinoa | 19 | Egg White Bites | 24 |
| Vanilla Quinoa | 20 | Crustless Mini Quiche Bites | 25 |
| Bacon & Veggie–Packed Frittatas | 20 | Gruyère Crustless Quiche | 25 |
| Beer-nana Loaf | 21 | Caramelised Vegetable Strata | 26 |
| Sausage Quinoa | 21 | | |

**27** Chapter 2 Soup, Chili and Stew

| | | | |
|---|---|---|---|
| Minestrone Soup | 27 | Sausage & Bean Soup | 32 |
| Sweet Potato & Wild Rice Chowder | 27 | Cheese Macaroni Soup | 33 |
| Mushroom Chicken Soup | 28 | Beef Reuben Soup | 33 |
| Chili Onion Mac | 28 | Enchilada Chicken Soup | 34 |
| Stuffed Potato Soup | 29 | Spicy Chicken | 35 |
| Chili without Bean | 29 | Vegetables & Chicken Breasts | 35 |
| Pork Stew with Tomatoes & Pinto Bean | 30 | Beef mince Stew | 36 |
| Healthy Black Bean Soup | 30 | Lamb Stew in Beef Stock | 36 |
| Chili Texas | 31 | Loaded Bacon Potato Soup | 37 |
| Cheese Squash Soup | 32 | Simple Firehouse Chili | 37 |

Table of Contents | 01

## 38　Chapter 3 Vegetables and Sides

| | | | |
|---|---|---|---|
| Barbecue Tofu Sandwiches | 38 | Pecan Bacon Strips | 45 |
| Broccoli with Garlic Dressing | 38 | Honey "Baked" Cauliflower | 46 |
| Middle Eastern Lentils & Rice | 39 | Cheese Broccoli Risotto | 46 |
| Flamboyant Flamenco Salad | 39 | Enchilada & Sweet Potato Casserole | 47 |
| Japanese-Style Vegetable Curry | 40 | Cheese Ravioli Casserole | 47 |
| Crispy Parmesan Polenta | 40 | Tomato Tortellini | 48 |
| Cannellini Beans with Tomatoes | 41 | Herb-Loaded Warm Potato Salad | 48 |
| Spiced Kidney Bean Stew | 42 | Stuffed Poblano Peppers | 49 |
| Red Lentil and Bulgur Soup | 43 | Chickpeas with Spinach | 49 |
| Curried Chickpeas with Coriander | 44 | Crustless Vegetable Potpie | 50 |
| Lentils & Bulgur | 45 | | |

## 51　Chapter 4 Poultry Mains

| | | | |
|---|---|---|---|
| Chicken Sausage Ragu | 51 | Tikka Chicken Masala | 57 |
| Chicken Sausage Gumbo | 52 | Orange Chicken Thighs & Vegetables | 58 |
| Chicken Lettuce Wraps | 52 | Carrot Chicken Tikka Masala | 59 |
| Pesto Chicken Pieces with Quinoa | 53 | Turkey Breast Roast in Chicken Stock | 59 |
| Veggie Chicken Casserole | 53 | Onion Chicken Shawarma | 60 |
| Duck Chunks with Potato Cubes | 54 | Turkey Breast with Vegetables | 61 |
| Garlic-Lemon Turkey Breast | 54 | Veggie & Duck Chunks | 61 |
| Tangy Thai Bash Orange Chicken | 55 | Chicken Scarpariello | 62 |
| Turkey Salsa Verde | 55 | Ketchup Chicken Wings | 63 |
| Mushroom & Chicken Chunk Stroganoff | 56 | Glazed Whole Turkey | 63 |
| Turkey Breast Casserole | 56 | Savory Turkey Wings | 64 |

## 65 Chapter 5 Seafood Mains

Onion Prawns Gumbo ..................... 65
Chipotle Salmon .......................... 66
Coconut Prawns .......................... 66
Red Curry Prawns ....................... 67
Cocktail Prawns .......................... 67
Thai Curry Salmon ....................... 68
Soy Salmon with Broccoli ............... 69
Celery Tuna Noodle Casserole........... 70
Quick Prawns Boil ....................... 70
Garlic-Chili Fish Tacos ................. 71
Honey-Garlic Salmon .................... 71
Pesto Tilapia with Sun-Dried Tomatoes  72
Old Bay-Seasoned Lobster Tails ........ 72
Brown Butter Pasta with Scallops &
  Tomatoes................................. 73
Scallop Risotto with Spinach ........... 73
Salmon with Zesty Dill Sauce ........... 74
Crab Legs with Lemon Wedges ......... 74

## 75 Chapter 6 Beef, Pork and Lamb

Mongolian Beef .......................... 75
Cheese Sandwiches ....................... 76
Herbed Pork Loin ........................ 76
Gravy Pork Chops with Onion........... 77
Pork Ragù ................................. 77
Mexican Beef Casserole ................. 78
Round Roast with Veggies .............. 78
Carrot Lamb Ragù ....................... 79
Feta Beef with Olives .................... 79
Barbecue Pulled Pork Sandwiches ...... 80
Stew Beef and Broccoli .................. 80
Beef Enchiladas .......................... 81
Italian Roast Ragù ....................... 82
Mozzarella Pork Chops ................. 82
Beef Bow-Ties in Spicy Tomato-Almond
  Sauce .................................... 83
Lamb Mince with Black Beans ......... 83
Cola Pulled Beef ......................... 84
Beef Meatloaf ............................ 84
Caribbean Pulled Pork ................... 85
Rosemary Lamb Cubes ................. 85
Red Wine Braised Beef Brisket ......... 86
Palatable Pork Tenderloin .............. 86
Beef Short Ribs with Carrots ........... 87
Honey Pork Chops ....................... 87
Mushroom Lamb Ragout................. 88
Potato Lamb Stew ....................... 88

Table of Contents | 03

## 89 Chapter 7 Desserts

| | | | | |
|---|---|---|---|---|
| Cranberry Stuffed Apples | 89 | Walnut Chocolate Brownies | 94 |
| Arroz Leche | 89 | Peaches with Cinnamon Whipped Cream | 95 |
| Tart Apple Comfort | 90 | Brownie Cake | 95 |
| Oats Stuffed Apples | 90 | Pearberry Crisp with Topping | 96 |
| Flan in Jar | 91 | Chocolate Custard | 96 |
| Typical Bread Pudding | 91 | Flavorful Crème Brûlée | 97 |
| Easy Black & Blue Cobbler | 92 | Baked Honey Plums | 97 |
| Vanilla Chocolate Custard | 92 | Apple Cobbler | 98 |
| Poached Pears | 93 | Lemon Mango Cake | 98 |
| Cinnamon Bananas Foster | 93 | Pumpkin-Spice Brown Rice Pudding | 99 |
| Classic Lava Cake | 94 | Butter Banana Cake | 99 |

## 100 Conclusion

## 101 Appendix Recipes Index

# Introduction

When you want home-cooked meals but are too lazy to make them yourself, the Ninja Foodi Max is an excellent purchase. It has 10 cooking capabilities built into its simple-to-use body, allowing you to roast, bake, grill, make crisp meals, and more, all while saving you time and energy. In reality, the Ninja Foodi MAX Multi-Cooker, as its full name suggests, can air fry food with up to 75% less fat than conventional techniques and pressure cook food up to 70% faster than conventional methods. Due to its enormous capacity, it is a fantastic choice for large families, but you will need enough countertop space or storage space to keep it. However, the curved body's black and stainless steel realization is fashionable. All the cooking settings are available on board in an easy-to-use digital display that may be operated with a single button click. With options like pressure cooking, steaming, grilling, air crisping without oil, baking, roasting, and dehydrating, your standard built-in oven may appear quite obsolete. In addition to a cook and crisp basket, there is a two-tier reversible rack for cooking main dishes and sides at the same time. This is useful for stacking veggies with meats, poultry, or fish. It has TenderCrisp Technology, which crisps food after cooking for an actual oven-cooked flavor. It's simple to throw ingredients into the Ninja and let it do its thing until it's time to eat. Use it to conjure up mouthwatering curries from Friday night fantasies or Sunday roasts that will solidify your position as the family cook to beat.

# Fundamentals of Ninja Foodi Max Multi-Cooker

## What is Ninja Foodi Max Multi-Cooker?

The old-fashioned iron devices with industrial-looking clamps on the side to prevent the lid from blowing off when the pressure grew too high and a steam valve on top that looked like a train whistle is not what we mean when we say "pressure cooker." We're referring to the slick, fashionable, and multipurpose digital appliances that are transforming kitchen cooking. Ninja Foodi Max is the best option here. This gadget is worth keeping on hand if you need dinner quickly because it can pressure cook 70% faster than conventional versions and can even prepare food from frozen. Without ever taking a cooking lesson, you can quickly and easily make wholesome family dinners with the Ninja Foodi MAX Multi-Cooker. Although having a large capacity is great from a family standpoint, many multi-cookers take a very long time to cook everything since they lack the raw power of a conventional oven. With the NINJA Foodi MAX Multi-Cooker, however, you can cook meals up to 70% quicker than with conventional appliances while still getting succulent, fall-off-the-bone meat thanks to the pressure cook mode. This monster can cook a 3-kilogram chicken in less than an hour, which should satisfy even the hungriest, anxious family members.

### Functions

Functions: From juicy steaks and delicately pulled pork to flavorful curries and flawlessly cooked pasta, pressure cooker meals are quick and delectable. Pressure cooking employs very hot steam to seal in liquids and may cook food up to 70% quicker than conventional methods.

1. STEAM:

When cooking delicate items at a high temperature, use steam. Healthy vegetable meals, tender asparagus, and elegant sea bass may all be steamed.

2. SLOW COOK:

Cook your meal more slowly and at

a lower temperature. Slow Warming casseroles, zesty risottos, and filling hotpots may all be prepared up to 12 hours ahead of time so that your supper is ready when you arrive home.

3. YOGURT:
Pasteurize milk and ferment it to make rich homemade yogurt.

4. SEAR/SAUTÉ:
Use the appliance as a cooktop to brown meats, sauté veggies, simmer sauces, and more.

5. AIR CRISP:
With up to 75% less fat than conventional frying techniques, Air Crisp may also be used as an air fryer to prepare meals and sides that require little to no oil, such as crispy fish fingers and chicken wings, and golden chips.

6. BAKE/ROAST:
For tender meats, baked goods, and other items, use the appliance as an oven. Roast succulent nut roasts, hearty vegetable medleys from the Mediterranean, and comforting winter vegetables. Make delicious treats, fresh bread, and cakes that you can be proud of.

7. GRILL:
Grill excellent burgers, salmon fillets, and a crispy topping for mac & cheese.

8. DEHYDRATE:
Dehydrate fruits, vegetables, and meats for wholesome snacking. To make nutritious dried fruit, such as mango, apple, strawberry, and bananas, as well as handmade root vegetable crisps, beef jerky, and dry herbs, dehydrate fresh ingredients.

9. KEEP WARM:
The appliance will automatically switch to the Keep Warm mode and begin

counting up after pressure cooking, steaming, or slow cooking. Keep Warm will stay on for 12 hours, or you may press KEEP WARM to turn it off. Keep Warm mode is not intended to warm food from a cold state but to keep it warm at a food-safe temperature.

## Step by Step Using It

### Air Crisp

1. Either put the Cook & Crisp Basket in the pot or the reversible rack. The basket should have a diffuser attached.
2. Add ingredients to the reversible rack or Cook & Crisp Basket. Put the lid on.
3. To choose AIR CRISP, spin the START/STOP dial after pressing FUNCTION. It will show the current temperature setting. To select a temperature between 150°C and 200°C, press TEMP and then spin the dial.
4. To change the cooking time in minute intervals up to an hour, press TIME and then spin the START/STOP dial.

Simply add 5 minutes to the cooking time to preheat your appliance. To start or stop cooking, press START/STOP.

5. If necessary, you may pull out the basket and open the lid while the food is cooking to shake or toss the contents for more equal browning. Close the cover after lowering the basket back into the pot. Once the lid is shut, cooking will automatically begin again.
6. The appliance will beep and show DONE when the cooking time is over.

### Grill

1. Either follow the instructions in your recipe or place the reversible rack in the pot in the upper grill position.
2. After arranging the items on the rack, secure the cover.
3. To choose GRILL, spin the START/STOP dial after pressing FUNCTION.
4. To change the cooking time in minute increments up to 30 minutes, press TIME and then turn the dial.
5. To start or stop cooking, press START/STOP.

4 | Fundamentals of Ninja Foodi Max Multi-Cooker

6. The appliance will beep and show DONE when the cooking time is over.

Bake/Roast

1. Fill the pot with the necessary materials and equipment. Put the lid on.
2. Select BAKE/ROAST by turning the START/STOP dial after pressing FUNCTION. It will show the current temperature setting. To choose a temperature between 120°C and 200°C, press TEMP and then spin the dial.
3. To change the cooking time, press TIME, then crank the START/STOP dial in minute increments up to 1 hour, then in 5-minute increments from 1 hour to 4 hours. To start or

stop cooking, press START/STOP.
4. The appliance will beep and show DONE when the cooking time is over.

Dehydrate

1. A layer of ingredients should be placed on the bottom position of the two-tier reversible rack in the pot.
2. Place the top layer over the reversible rack as shown below, holding it in place with its grips. After that, add an ingredient layer to the top tier and secure the lid.
3. Select DEHYDRATE by turning the START/STOP dial after pressing FUNCTION. It will show the current temperature setting. To select a temperature between 40°C and 90°C, press TEMP and then spin the dial.
4. Press TIME, then spin the dial to change the cooking time up to 12 hours in 15-minute intervals.
5. To start the dehydration process, close the lid and press START/STOP.
6. The appliance will beep and show DONE when the cooking time is over.

Pressure Cook

1. Place the pot in the cooker base and add 750ml of room-temperature water to the pot.
2. By lining up the arrow on the front of the lid with the arrow on the front of the cooker base, you can assemble the pressure lid. When the lid latches into place, spin it clockwise.
3. A pressure release valve should be in the SEAL position.
4. Press FUNCTION, then choose PRESSURE by using the START/STOP dial. High (HI) pressure and a 2-minute time setting are the default

settings for the device. To start, press START/STOP.

5. The display's PRE and some steam leakage suggest there is increasing pressure. The countdown will start once the pressure is at its maximum.
6. The device will beep and show DONE after the countdown before automatically entering KEEP WARM mode and starting the counting up.
7. To quickly discharge the pressurized steam, turn the pressure release valve to the VENT position. The pressure release valve will discharge a blast of steam. The float valve will drop after all of the steam has been released, allowing the lid to be opened.

**Steam**

1. The reversible rack or Cook & Crisp Basket with ingredients should be placed in the pot after adding 250 ml of liquid (or the quantity suggested by the recipe).
2. Turn the pressure release valve to the VENT position after installing the pressure lid.
3. Press FUNCTION, then choose STEAM using the START/STOP dial.
4. To change the cooking time in minute increments up to 30 minutes, press TIME and then turn the dial. To start or stop cooking, press START/STOP.
5. To get the liquid to boil, the machine will start preheating. PRE will

appear on the screen. The preheating image will play until the appliance reaches the desired temperature, at which point BOIL will appear on the display and the timer will start to clock down.
6. The appliance will automatically switch to Keep Warm mode and start counting up once the cooking time is up by beeping. Before opening the lid, be sure the float valve has descended.

**Slow Cook**

1. Add all components to the pot. The pot should not be filled past the MAX line.
2. Turn the pressure release valve to the VENT position after installing the pressure lid.
3. Press FUNCTION, then choose SLOW COOK using the START/STOP dial. It will show the current temperature setting. To choose HI or LO, spin the dial after pressing TEMP.
4. Press TIME, then spin the dial to change the cooking time up to 12 hours in 15-minute intervals.

4. To start or stop cooking, press START/STOP.
6. The appliance will beep, go into Keep Warm mode, and start counting up once the cooking time is up.

**Yogurt**

1. Add milk to the saucepan in the required quantity.
2. Turn the pressure release valve to the VENT position after installing the pressure lid.
3. To choose YOGURT, spin the START/STOP dial after pressing FUNCTION. It will show the current temperature setting. Press TEMP, then choose YGRT or FMNT using the dial.
4. Press TIME, and then move the dial to change the incubation time between 8 and 12 hours in 30-minute intervals.
5. To start pasteurization, press START/STOP. 6 While pasteurizing, the unit will display "BOIL." The device will beep and indicate "COOL" when the pasteurization temperature has been reached.
6. The device will show ADD and STIR in sequence along with the incubation period after the milk has cooled.
7. Remove the pressure lid, then skim the milk's surface.
8. Stir milk and yogurt cultures together. To start the incubation process, attach the pressure lid and click START/STOP.
9. The countdown will start after FMNT appears on the display. The device will beep and display DONE when the incubation period is finished. Until it is turned off, the device will beep once per minute for up to four

hours.

10. Up to 12 hours before serving, chill yogurt.

### Sear/Sauté

1. Add ingredients to the pot.
2. Select SEAR/SAUTÉ by turning the dial after pressing FUNCTION. It will show the current temperature setting. Press TEMP, then choose LO, LO: MD, MD, MD: HI, or HI by rotating the dial.
3. To start or stop cooking, press START/STOP.
4. To switch off the SEAR/SAUTÉ feature, press START/STOP. Press FUNCTION, then rotate the START/STOP dial to the appropriate cooking function to change the cooking function.

### Pressure Release Options

Natural Pressure Release: As the appliance cools down after pressure cooking is finished, steam will naturally escape from it. Depending on the number of components in the pot, this might take up to 20 minutes. The appliance will then enter the Keep Warm mode. If you want to exit Keep Warm mode, press KEEP WARM. The float valve will descend when the whole natural pressure release has occurred.

Only use a quick pressure release if your recipe specifies it. Turn the pressure release valve to the VENT position to swiftly release the steam after pressure cooking and the KEEP WARM light turns on. An audible hiss will be present when steam is released. After the pressure is released, some steam will still be within the appliance, but it will eventually leak when the lid is opened. Make sure there are no condensation drips in the stove base when you lift and tilt it away from you.

### Extra Accessories for Perfect Cooking in Ninja Foodi Max Multi-Cooker:

1. Cooking Pot: An additional pot to continue the Foodi® fun when your primary pot is already brimming with delectable food.
2. Multi-Purpose Silicone Sling: Easily pull ingredients and pans into and out of the cooking pot with the Multi-Purpose Silicone Sling.
3. Multi-Purpose Tin: Bake a fluffy, moist cake with a golden top for dessert, or make casseroles, dips, and sweet or savory pies. H6cm D22cm.
4. Folding Crisping Rack: Make taco shells out of tortillas or cook a

8 | Fundamentals of Ninja Foodi Max Multi-Cooker

complete package of bacon.

5. Our particularly sized loaf pan is the ideal baking tool for bread mixtures like banana and courgette. approx. L21cm x W11cm x H9cm.
6. Glass lid: Use it to effortlessly carry or store food while cooking and to see inside the pot.
7. Additional Pack of Silicone Rings: Use one silicone ring while cooking savory meals and the other when cooking sweet items to help maintain flavours distinct.
8. Skewer Stand: Only the 7.5L variants are compatible with the skewer stand. Make kebabs with the skewer stand. Included are 15 skewers.

## Cleaning

- After each usage, the appliance has to be completely cleaned.
- Before cleaning, unplug the device from the electrical socket.
- Wipe a moist towel over the control panel and stove base to clean them.
- Dishwasher-safe items include the pressure lid, cooking pot, silicone ring, reversible rack, Cook & Crisp Basket, and detachable diffuser.
- The anti-clog cap and pressure release valve may be cleaned with water and dish soap.
- After the heat shield has cooled, clean the crisping lid by wiping it down with a wet cloth or paper towel.
- Fill the pot with water and let it soak before cleaning if food residue is stuck to the cooking pot, reversible rack, or Cook & Crisp Basket. AVOID using scouring pads. If scrubbing is required, use a nylon pad or brush with liquid dish soap or non-abrasive cleaner.
- After each usage, let all pieces air dry.

### Taking Off and Replacing the Silicone Ring

- Pull the silicone ring piece by section outward from the silicone ring rack to remove it. Either side of the ring can be mounted facing upward. Section by section, push it into the rack to reinstall. Remove any food particles from the silicone ring and anti-clog

Fundamentals of Ninja Foodi Max Multi-Cooker | 9

cap after use.
- To prevent odor, keep the silicone ring clean. The smell may be eliminated by washing it in the dishwasher or warm, soapy water. It is nonetheless typical for it to take in the aroma of some acidic meals. It is advised to keep several silicone rings on hand.
- NEVER take the silicone ring out too forcefully as this might damage the rack and the pressure-sealing ability. Replace any silicone ring that has cracks, cuts, or other damage right away.

### Frequently Asked Questions

**1. Why does it take my unit so long to reach pressure? How long does it take for pressure to build?**
- Depending on the chosen temperature, the cooking pot's current temperature, and the temperature or amount of the contents, cooking durations may vary.
- Make sure your silicone ring is flat with the lid and properly placed. If placed properly, you should be able to spin the ring by giving it a small tug.
- When pressure cooking, make sure the pressure lid is completely closed and the pressure release valve is in the SEAL position.

**2. Why does the clock go so slowly?**
- Instead of setting minutes, you may have done so. When setting the time, the display will read HH: MM and the time will advance or backward by minutes.

**3. How can I detect whether the appliance is under pressure?**
- As the device builds pressure, whirling lights will show up on the screen. When utilizing the pressure or steam function, PRE and moving lights are displayed on the display screen.
- When utilizing STEAM or

10 | Fundamentals of Ninja Foodi Max Multi-Cooker

PRESSURE, this shows that the unit is building pressure or preheating. Your designated cook time will start to run out once the machine has completed creating pressure.
- It's usual for steam to leak through the pressure release valve while cooking.
- There is a lot of steam coming from my device when utilizing the Steam feature. For steam, slow cooking, and sear/sauté, keep the pressure release valve in the VENT position.

**4. Why am I unable to remove the pressure lid?**
- The pressure cover won't unlock as a safety measure until the device is fully depressurized. To quickly discharge the pressurized steam, turn the pressure release valve to the VENT position. Steam will suddenly erupt from the pressure release valve. The appliance will be prepared to open after all of the steam has been released. Turn the pressure lid counterclockwise, then lift the lid at an angle to prevent splatter. Do not lift the lid straight up.

**5. Is the pressure release valve supposed to be loose?**
- Yes. The loose fit of the pressure release valve is deliberate; it makes it simple to switch from SEAL to VENT and helps manage pressure by releasing a tiny quantity of steam while cooking to provide excellent results. For pressure cooking, please

make sure it is turned as far as possible toward the SEAL position, and for rapid releasing, please make sure it is turned as far as possible toward the VENT position. The appliance hisses and cannot build pressure. A pressure release valve should be switched to the SEAL setting, so double-check this. If, after doing this, if you still hear a loud hissing sound, your silicone seal might not be installed completely. To stop cooking, press START/STOP, vent as required, and take off the pressure cover. Make sure the silicone ring is properly placed and flatly underneath the ring rack by applying pressure to it. Once everything is in place, you ought to be able to spin the ring by giving it a gentle tug. Instead of ticking down, the device is counting up.
- The appliance is in Keep Warm mode after the cooking cycle has finished.

**6. How much time does it take the unit to depressurize?**
- A quick release lasts no more than

two minutes. Depending on the type of food, amount of liquid, and/or combination of food and liquid in the pot, natural release can take up to 20 minutes or more.

**7. The error message "ADD POT" displays on the monitor.**
- The cooker base does not contain the cooking pot. Every function requires a cooking pot.

**8. The error message "OTHR LID" and the lid icon flash on the display screen.**
- The wrong lid is attached for the cooking operation you want. To utilize the Pressure, Slow Cook, Yogurt, Steam, or Keep Warm features, install the pressure lid.

**9. The error message "SHUT LID" shows on the monitor.**
- The desired function cannot begin because the crisping lid is open.

**10. The error message "TURN LID" displays on the monitor.**
- The pressure lid's installation is incomplete. To utilize the pressure, slow cook, yogurt, steam, and keep warm features, turn the pressure knob clockwise until it clicks.

**11. The problem message "OPEN VENT" displays on the display panel.**
- The pressure release valve is in the SEAL position when the device is set to Slow Cook or Sear/Sauté and detects pressure building up.
- For the duration of the cooking operation, turn the pressure release valve to the VENT position and leave it there.
- The program will end and the device will switch off if the pressure release valve is not turned to the VENT position in the allotted time of five minutes.

**12. When utilizing the Steam feature,**

**a notice titled "ADD WATR" shows on the screen.**
- The water is not deep enough. To keep the device functioning, add extra water.

13. **An error message with the text "ADD WATR" appears on the screen while using the Pressure function.**
- Before starting the pressure cook cycle again, add extra liquid to the cooking pot.
- A pressure release valve should be in the SEAL position.
- Verify that the silicone ring is properly fitted.

## Cooking Tips and Warnings

1. For uniform browning, ensure sure components are layered evenly and without overlap in the bottom of the cooking pot. If components overlap, shake the pan halfway during the cooking period.
2. We advise first wrapping tiny items in a parchment paper or foil bag if they could fall through the reversible rack.
3. For maximum crisping results, it is advised to drain the pot of any liquid before switching from pressure cooking to using the crisping cover.
4. After cooking, maintain food at a warm, safe temperature by using the Keep Warm option. We advise keeping the lid on and using this feature right before serving to avoid food drying out. Use the Air Crisp option to reheat food and NEVER use the socket under the counter.
5. NEVER attach this appliance to a separate remote control or timer switch.
6. If the plug or power cable is damaged, do not use the appliance. Stop using the appliance right away and contact customer service if it has any problems or has been damaged in any way.
7. To protect yourself from steam and hot liquids, ALWAYS tilt the lid so that it is between your body and the inside pot.
8. ALWAYS make sure the appliance is installed correctly before using it.
9. Always inspect the red float valve and pressure release valve for blockage or clogging before using, and clean them if required. Verify that the pressure lid's red float valve can move easily. When cooked under pressure, foods like apple sauce, cranberries, pearl

Fundamentals of Ninja Foodi Max Multi-Cooker | 13

barley, oatmeal or other cereals, split peas, noodles, macaroni, rhubarb, or spaghetti may foam, froth, or sputter, blocking the pressure release valve.

10. NEVER use the SLOW COOK option if there is no food or liquid in the detachable cooking pot.
11. The use of the device without the cooking pot is not recommended.
12. DO NOT deep fried anything in this appliance.
13. The pressure valves MUST NOT be covered.
14. While pressure cooking, AVOID using oil for sautéing or frying.
15. Keep food away from hot sources. When cooking, DO NOT overfill or go over the MAX load level. Overfilling might endanger users' safety, result in property damage, or render the appliance unsafe.
16. DO NOT overfill the Cook & Crisp Basket to keep food from coming into touch with the heating components.

17. Close the crisping lid very carefully to avoid trapping anything in the hinge or getting it hooked.
18. Different socket voltages may have an impact on how well your product functions. Use a thermometer to ensure that your food is prepared to the proper temperatures to avoid any potential illnesses.
19. When operating, DO NOT position the appliance close to a worktop edge.
20. Avoid using metal scouring pads when cleaning. An electric shock risk exists if broken pieces of the pad come into contact with electrical components.
21. NEVER handle kitchen utensils while cooking or just after.

# 4-Week Meal Plan

## Week 1

**Day 1:**
Breakfast: Taco Huevos Rancheros
Lunch: Broccoli with Garlic Dressing
Dinner: Chicken Sausage Ragu
Dessert: Tart Apple Comfort

**Day 2:**
Breakfast: Spanish Tortilla with Sauce
Lunch: Middle Eastern Lentils & Rice
Dinner: Mexican Beef Casserole
Dessert: Easy Black & Blue Cobbler

**Day 3:**
Breakfast: Spinach Eggs Florentine
Lunch: Barbecue Tofu Sandwiches
Dinner: Pesto Chicken Pieces with Quinoa
Dessert: Flan in Jar

**Day 4:**
Breakfast: Easy Breads
Lunch: Japanese-Style Vegetable Curry
Dinner: Herbed Pork Loin
Dessert: Poached Pears

**Day 5:**
Breakfast: Beer-nana Loaf
Lunch: Crispy Parmesan Polenta
Dinner: Carrot Lamb Ragù
Dessert: Classic Lava Cake

**Day 6:**
Breakfast: Crescent Rolls
Lunch: Cannellini Beans with Tomatoes
Dinner: Tangy Thai Bash Orange Chicken
Dessert: Cranberry Stuffed Apples

**Day 7:**
Breakfast: Enchilada Casserole
Lunch: Spiced Kidney Bean Stew
Dinner: Gravy Pork Chops with Onion
Dessert: Arroz Leche

## Week 2

**Day 1:**
Breakfast: Egg White Bites
Lunch: Red Lentil and Bulgur Soup
Dinner: Mushroom & Chicken Chunk Stroganoff
Dessert: Typical Bread Pudding

**Day 2:**
Breakfast: Crustless Mini Quiche Bites
Lunch: Curried Chickpeas with Coriander
Dinner: Mongolian Beef
Dessert: Vanilla Chocolate Custard

**Day 3:**
Breakfast: Gruyère Crustless Quiche
Lunch: Lentils & Bulgur
Dinner: Onion Prawns Gumbo
Dessert: Oats Stuffed Apples

**Day 4:**
Breakfast: Bacon & Veggie-Packed Frittatas
Lunch: Flamboyant Flamenco Salad
Dinner: Garlic-Lemon Turkey Breast
Dessert: Peaches with Cinnamon Whipped Cream

**Day 5:**
Breakfast: Caramelised Vegetable Strata
Lunch: Pecan Bacon Strips
Dinner: Caribbean Pulled Pork
Dessert: Brownie Cake

**Day 6:**
Breakfast: Vanilla Quinoa
Lunch: Honey "Baked" Cauliflower
Dinner: Glazed Whole Turkey
Dessert: Pearberry Crisp with Topping

**Day 7:**
Breakfast: Almond Cranberry Quinoa
Lunch: Enchilada & Sweet Potato Casserole
Dinner: Orange Chicken Thighs & Vegetables
Dessert: Flavorful Crème Brûlée

## Week 3

### Day 1:
Breakfast: Millet Porridge
Lunch: Cheese Broccoli Risotto
Dinner: Red Wine Braised Beef Brisket
Dessert: Apple Cobbler

### Day 2:
Breakfast: Lemon-Seasoned Quinoa
Lunch: Cheese Ravioli Casserole
Dinner: Carrot Chicken Tikka Masala
Dessert: Cinnamon Bananas Foster

### Day 3:
Breakfast: Sausage Quinoa
Lunch: Tomato Tortellini
Dinner: Turkey Breast with Vegetables
Dessert: Pumpkin-Spice Brown Rice Pudding

### Day 4:
Breakfast: Taco Huevos Rancheros
Lunch: Chickpeas with Spinach
Dinner: Thai Curry Salmon
Dessert: Cranberry Stuffed Apples

### Day 5:
Breakfast: Spinach Eggs Florentine
Lunch: Herb-Loaded Warm Potato Salad
Dinner: Stew Beef and Broccoli
Dessert: Chocolate Custard

### Day 6:
Breakfast: Spanish Tortilla with Sauce
Lunch: Stuffed Poblano Peppers
Dinner: Ketchup Chicken Wings
Dessert: Baked Honey Plums

### Day 7:
Breakfast: Easy Breads
Lunch: Crustless Vegetable Potpie
Dinner: Honey Pork Chops
Dessert: Walnut Chocolate Brownies

## Week 4

### Day 1:
Breakfast: Beer-nana Loaf
Lunch: Cheese Squash Soup
Dinner: Celery Tuna Noodle Casserole
Dessert: Lemon Mango Cake

### Day 2:
Breakfast: Crescent Rolls
Lunch: Middle Eastern Lentils & Rice
Dinner: Rosemary Lamb Cubes
Dessert: Tart Apple Comfort

### Day 3:
Breakfast: Enchilada Casserole
Lunch: Healthy Black Bean Soup
Dinner: Pesto Tilapia with Sun-Dried Tomatoes
Dessert: Easy Black & Blue Cobbler

### Day 4:
Breakfast: Egg White Bites
Lunch: Red Lentil and Bulgur Soup
Dinner: Feta Beef with Olives
Dessert: Butter Banana Cake

### Day 5:
Breakfast: Crustless Mini Quiche Bites
Lunch: Broccoli with Garlic Dressing
Dinner: Salmon with Zesty Dill Sauce
Dessert: Poached Pears

### Day 6:
Breakfast: Gruyère Crustless Quiche
Lunch: Cannellini Beans with Tomatoes
Dinner: Mushroom Lamb Ragout
Dessert: Classic Lava Cake

### Day 7:
Breakfast: Bacon & Veggie–Packed Frittatas
Lunch: Flamboyant Flamenco Salad
Dinner: Veggie Chicken Casserole
Dessert: Vanilla Chocolate Custard

# Chapter 1 Breakfast

## Taco Huevos Rancheros

**Prep Time:** 10 minutes | **Cook Time:** 20 minutes | **Serves:** 4

220 g dried pinto beans, picked over and soaked overnight or quick-soaked
4 teaspoons taco seasoning, plus more for garnish
235 g tomato salsa
**Optional garnishes**
Sour cream
Chopped fresh coriander

Salt and freshly ground black pepper
4 large eggs
4 (15 cm) corn tortillas, warmed, or 4 handfuls tortilla chips

Grated pepper Jack cheese

1. Drain the beans. 2. Stir the beans, 360 ml water and the taco seasoning in the pot. 3. Close the lid, turn the pressure release valve to SEAL position, and then move the slider to PRESSURE. 4. Select HI and set the cooking time to 7 minutes. 5. Press START/STOP to begin cooking. 6. When finished, release the pressure quickly. 7. Drain off most of the cooking liquid from the beans and discard. Return the beans in the pot to the appliance, stir in the salsa, and then season them with salt and pepper. 8. Use a wooden spoon to create four indentations in the beans. Carefully crack the eggs into the indentations, and sprinkle the eggs with a few pinches of taco seasoning. 9. Cover the lid and use the dial to select SEAR/SAUTÉ. Select Lo2, and then press START/STOP to begin cooking. Cook them for 5 minutes until the egg whites are just set and the yolks are still runny. Remove the pot from the appliance. 10. Place the tortillas or tortilla chips on plates. Carefully scoop up the eggs and beans and place them on top of the tortillas or chips. Serve the dish immediately, and you can serve with the garnishes, if desired.
**Per Serving:** Calories 317; Fat: 6.7g; Sodium: 303mg; Carbs: 44.77g; Fibre: 10g; Sugar: 2.73g; Protein: 19.25g

## Spanish Tortilla with Sauce

**Prep Time:** 25 minutes | **Cook Time:** 20 minutes | **Serves:** 4

2 tablespoons olive oil
½ medium yellow onion, thinly sliced
1 large (300 g) russet potato, peeled and cut into 1 cm
Salt and freshly ground black pepper
8 large eggs
½ teaspoon smoked paprika
150 g drained jarred roasted red peppers

1. Spray a suitable baking pan with cooking spray and line the bottom with a round of parchment paper; spray the parchment with the cooking spray as well. 2. Add the oil to the pot; use the dial to select SEAR/SAUTÉ. Select Lo3, and then press START/STOP to begin cooking. 3. When the oil is hot, add the onion and cook for 3 minutes until beginning to soften; add the potato, 1 teaspoon salt, and several grinds of pepper and stir them to combine. Cover the lid loosely and cook them for 4 to 5 minutes until the potatoes are barely tender when pierced with a fork. Stop the process. 4. Scrape the onion and potato into the prepared baking pan. 5. In a small bowl, whisk together the eggs with ¼ teaspoon of the paprika. Pour the egg mixture into the baking pan over the potato mixture. 6. Pour 360 ml water into the pot and place the rack in the pot; place the baking pan on the rack. 7. Close the lid, turn the pressure release valve to SEAL position, and then move the slider to PRESSURE. 8. Select HI and set the cooking time to 10 minutes. 9. Press START/STOP to begin cooking. 10. When finished, release the pressure naturally. 11. Blend the roasted peppers with the remaining ¼ teaspoon smoked paprika and a few grinds of pepper until smooth. Set aside. 12. Carefully remove the pan from the pot. 13. Run a knife around the edges of the pan, place a dinner plate over the pan, and carefully invert the tortilla onto the plate. 14. Cut the tortilla into wedges and serve with the sauce.

**Per Serving:** Calories 293; Fat: 16.47g; Sodium: 148mg; Carbs: 21.46g; Fibre: 2.1g; Sugar: 3.04g; Protein: 15.1g

## Millet Porridge

**Prep Time:** 5 minutes | **Cook Time:** 10 minutes | **Serves:** 2

75 g millet
240 ml water
Salt to taste
Butter to taste, optional

1. Mix the millet and water in the pot and stir. Add salt to taste. 2. Close the lid, turn the pressure release valve to SEAL position, and then move the slider to PRESSURE. Select HI and set the cooking time to 8 minutes. Press START/STOP to begin cooking. When finished, release the pressure naturally. 3. Open the lid and fluff the millet with a fork before serving. If you like, you can add butter to taste.

**Per Serving:** Calories 189; Fat: 2.11g; Sodium: 82mg; Carbs: 36.43g; Fibre: 4.3g; Sugar: 0g; Protein: 5.51g

## Spinach Eggs Florentine

**Prep Time:** 10 minutes | **Cook Time:** 30 minutes | **Serves:** 4

1 tablespoon olive oil
2 medium garlic cloves, chopped
125 g baby spinach
Salt and freshly ground black pepper
360 g cottage cheese
5 large eggs
40 g – 75 g crumbled feta cheese
2 tablespoons chopped fresh dill

1. Spray a suitable baking pan with cooking spray and set aside. 2. Add the oil to the pot, then use the dial to select SEAR/SAUTÉ. Select Lo3, and then press START/STOP to begin cooking. 3. When the oil is hot, add the garlic and cook for 30 seconds until fragrant; add the spinach, 2 teaspoons water, a few pinches of salt, and several grinds of pepper, and then cook them for 2 minutes until wilted. 4. Stop the process, transfer the spinach and garlic to a mesh strainer and press with a wooden spoon to extract as much liquid as possible. 5. Stir the spinach mixture with the cottage cheese in a bowl until combined; add the eggs, feta cheese, dill, ½ teaspoon salt and a few grinds of pepper, and whisk them combine. 6. Transfer the egg mixture to the prepared baking pan and cover the pan tightly with foil. 7. Add 360 ml water to the pot, then place in the rack and place the baking pan on the rack. 8. Close the lid, turn the pressure release valve to SEAL position, and then move the slider to PRESSURE. 9. Select HI and set the cooking time to 25 minutes. 10. Press START/STOP to begin cooking. 11. When finished, release the pressure naturally. Blot the excess water from the top of the foil with paper towels. Remove the baking pan from the pot and carefully uncover. The eggs are done when a knife inserted into the centre comes out clean with no liquid egg clinging to the knife. 12. Let the dish sit for 5 minutes and then cut into wedges and serve.
**Per Serving:** Calories 240; Fat: 15.15g; Sodium: 462mg; Carbs: 6.96g; Fibre: 1.5g; Sugar: 2.67g; Protein: 19.63g

## Lemon-Seasoned Quinoa

**Prep Time:** 10 minutes | **Cook Time:** 5 minutes | **Serves:** 2-4

325 g quinoa
720 ml water or vegetable stock
Juice of 1 lemon
½ tsp. salt
Handful your choice of fresh herbs, minced

1. Rinse the quinoa well. 2. Add the quinoa, stock, lemon juice, salt, and herbs (optional) into the pot. 3. Close the lid, turn the pressure release valve to SEAL position, and then move the slider to PRESSURE. Select HI and set the cooking time to 1 minute. Press START/STOP to begin cooking. When finished, release the pressure naturally. 4. Carefully unlock the lid and fluff the cooked quinoa with a fork. 5. Serve.
**Per Serving:** Calories 324; Fat: 5.19g; Sodium: 707mg; Carbs: 57.62g; Fibre: 6g; Sugar: 1.8g; Protein: 12.04g

## Vanilla Quinoa

**Prep Time:** 10 minutes | **Cook Time:** 5 minutes | **Serves:** 4-6

250 g quinoa, uncooked, well rinsed
2 tbsp. maple syrup
¼ tsp. ground cinnamon
**Optional toppings:**
Sliced almonds
Fresh berries
½ tsp. vanilla
540 ml water
A pinch of salt

Milk

1. Rinse the quinoa well. 2. Combine all ingredients in the pot and lock the lid. 3. Turn the pressure release valve to SEAL position, and then move the slider to PRESSURE. Select HI and set the cooking time to 1 minute. Press START/STOP to begin cooking. When finished, release the pressure naturally. 4. Unlock the lid. Fluff the cooked quinoa with a fork. 5. Serve the quinoa with almonds, milk, and berries (optional).
**Per Serving:** Calories 263; Fat: 3.88g; Sodium: 46mg; Carbs: 47.81g; Fibre: 4.6g; Sugar: 6.12g; Protein: 9.01g

## Bacon & Veggie-Packed Frittatas

**Prep Time:** 20 minutes | **Cook Time:** 15 minutes | **Serves:** 4

2 tbsp. grass-fed butter or ghee, plus more for jars
35 g cleaned and thinly sliced white button or cremini mushrooms
1 large celery rib, thinly sliced
15 g prewashed finely chopped fresh spinach
6 large eggs
60 ml milk of choice
½ tsp. sea salt
½ tsp. garlic granules or garlic powder
¼ tsp. onion powder
¼ tsp. dried thyme
2 tbsp chopped fresh flat-leaf parsley, plus more for garnish
60 g shredded sharp or mild cheddar cheese
20 g shredded Parmesan, provolone or Gruyère cheese
4 slices cooked crispy bacon, crumbled
355 ml water

1. Select SEAR/SAUTÉ. Select Lo3, and then press START/STOP to begin cooking. 2. When the pot is hot, melt the healthy fat you chose; add the mushrooms and celery, and sauté them for 7 minutes until lightly caramelized; add the spinach and sauté for 2 minutes or just until wilted. Stop the process. 3. Butter 4 wide-mouth ramekins. Set them aside. 4. In a large bowl, whisk together the eggs and your milk of choice until the eggs are fully incorporated. Add the sautéed veggies, salt, garlic granules, onion powder, thyme, parsley, shredded cheeses and crumbled bacon. 5. Evenly pour the mixture into the prepared ramekins, and cover the tops of the ramekins with unbleached parchment paper, then top them with foil and secure it around the edges. 6. Pour the water into the pot and place the rack in it, and then place the ramekins on the rack. 7. Close the lid, turn the pressure release valve to SEAL position, and then move the slider to PRESSURE. Select HI and set the cooking time to 5 minutes. Press START/STOP to begin cooking. When finished, release the pressure naturally. 8. Allow the frittatas to rest for 5 minutes before serving.
**Per Serving:** Calories 362; Fat: 28.68g; Sodium: 712mg; Carbs: 6.01g; Fibre: 1.1g; Sugar: 1.95g; Protein: 20.11g

## Beer-nana Loaf

**Prep Time:** 15 minutes | **Cook Time:** 55 minutes | **Serves:** 1 loaf

370 g self-rising flour
60 g quick-cooking oats
105 g packed brown sugar
3 medium mashed ripe bananas
1 bottle (300 ml.) wheat beer

60 g maple syrup
2 tbsp. olive oil
1 tbsp. sesame seeds
¼ tsp. salt

1. Mix the flour, oats and brown sugar in a large bowl. 2. Mix the bananas, beer and maple syrup in another bowl until blended. Add to the flour mixture; stir them just until moistened. 3. Transfer the mixture to a greased loaf pan; drizzle the mixture with oil and sprinkle with sesame seeds and salt. 4. Add the loaf pan to the pot. Close the lid and move slider to AIR FRY/STOVETOP, then use the dial to select BAKE/ROAST. Adjust the cooking temperature to 190°C and set the cooking time to 60 minutes. Press START/STOP to begin cooking. 5. A toothpick inserted in centre should come out clean when cooked. 6. Cool the load in pan for 10 minutes before removing to wire rack to cool.

**Per Serving:** Calories 678; Fat: 11.75g; Sodium: 1280mg; Carbs: 126.47g; Fibre: 4.4g; Sugar: 43.31g; Protein: 11.62g

## Sausage Quinoa

**Prep Time:** 15 minutes | **Cook Time:** 5 minutes | **Serves:** 2-4

1 tbsp. olive oil
225 g sausage meat, casings removed
1 small yellow onion, chopped
A pinch of turmeric powder
½ tsp. sweet paprika

240 ml chicken stock
170 g quinoa
1 red pepper , chopped
25 g. Bella mushrooms, halved
½ small broccoli head, florets separated

1. Select SEAR/SAUTÉ. Select Lo3, and then press START/STOP to begin cooking. 2. When the pot is hot, add the oil, sausage and onion, stir and brown them for a few minutes; stir in the turmeric, paprika, stock, quinoa, mushrooms and pepper , and then stop this process. 3. Close the lid, turn the pressure release valve to SEAL position, and then move the slider to PRESSURE. Select HI and set the cooking time to 1 minute. Press START/STOP to begin cooking. When finished, release the pressure naturally. 4. Open the lid and fluff the cooked quinoa with a fork. 5. Serve.

**Per Serving:** Calories 370; Fat: 16.57g; Sodium: 740mg; Carbs: 41.43g; Fibre: 6g; Sugar: 1.81g; Protein: 18.12g

## Crescent Rolls

**Prep Time:** 40 minutes | **Cook Time:** 10 minutes | **Serves:** 8

370- 430 g plain flour
2 pkg. (5 g each) active dry yeast
1 tsp. salt
240 ml whole milk
110 g butter, cubed
60 g honey
3 large egg yolks
2 tbsp. butter, melted

1. Combine 180 g flour, yeast and salt in a bowl. 2. In a small saucepan, heat milk, cubed butter and honey to 50°C. 3. Add the liquid to dry ingredients; beat them on medium speed for 2 minutes; add the egg yolks, and beat them again on high for 2 minutes; stir in enough remaining flour to form soft dough. 4. Turn dough onto a floured surface; knead the dough for 6 to 8 minutes until smooth and elastic. 5. Place the kneaded dough in a greased bowl, turning once to grease the top. Cover the bowl with plastic wrap and let rise in a warm place for about 45 minutes or until doubled. 6. Punch down dough; place it in a resealable plastic bag. Seal and refrigerate it overnight. 7. Turn dough onto a lightly floured surface and divide in half. Roll each portion into a 36 cm. circle; cut each circle into 16 wedges. Lightly brush wedges with melted butter. Roll them up from wide ends, pinching pointed ends to seal. 8. Line a baking sheet with parchment paper, and transfer the rolls to it with point side down; cover the baking sheet with lightly greased plastic wrap, and then let them rise in a warm place for 45 minutes or until doubled. 9. After that, transfer the baking sheet to the pot. Close the lid and move slider to AIR FRY/STOVETOP, then use the dial to select BAKE/ROAST. Adjust the cooking temperature to 190°Cand set the cooking time to 11 minutes. Press START/STOP to begin cooking. 10. Serve warm.
**Per Serving:** Calories 427; Fat: 17.73g; Sodium: 424mg; Carbs: 58.36g; Fibre: 2.1g; Sugar: 12.82g; Protein: 8.87g

## Almond Cranberry Quinoa

**Prep Time:** 5 minutes | **Cook Time:** 10 minutes | **Serves:** 2-4

480 ml water
170 g quinoa
130 g dried cranberries
65 g slivered almonds
30 g salted sunflower seeds

1. Rinse the quinoa well. 2. Combine water and quinoa in the pot. 3. Close the lid, turn the pressure release valve to SEAL position, and then move the slider to PRESSURE. Select HI and set the cooking time to 10 minutes. Press START/STOP to begin cooking. When finished, release the pressure quickly. 4. Add sunflower seeds, almonds, and dried cranberries to the quinoa, and gently mix them until well combined. 5. Serve.
**Per Serving:** Calories 290; Fat: 11.55g; Sodium: 59mg; Carbs: 39.58g; Fibre: 3.9g; Sugar: 9.2g; Protein: 8.8g

## Enchilada Casserole

**Prep Time:** 35 minutes | **Cook Time:** 25 minutes | **Serves:** 4-6

240 ml water
1 tbsp. extra-virgin olive oil
20 small flour tortillas
170 g cooked breakfast sausage links, diced
1 red pepper, seeded and stemmed and thinly sliced
½ yellow onion, thinly sliced
85 g drained and rinsed canned black beans
175 ml canned red enchilada sauce
4 large eggs
1 tsp. heavy cream
¼ tsp. dried oregano
¼ tsp. crushed red pepper flakes
Salt
Freshly ground black pepper
175 g shredded Mexican-blend cheese

1. Coat a suitable baking pan with olive oil. Arrange 2 or 3 tortillas on the bottom of the pan, enough to cover the bottom. 2. Place ⅓ of the sausage, ⅓ of the sliced red pepper, ⅓ of the sliced onion and ⅓ of the black beans on top of the tortillas; top them with 2 to 3 tablespoons of the enchilada sauce. 3. Mix the eggs, cream, oregano, red pepper flakes, salt and black pepper in a small bowl. Pour ⅓ of the egg mixture over the veggie- and bean-topped tortilla. Sprinkle a big pinch of cheese over the eggs and then top with 2 or 3 more tortillas. 4. Do the same with the next two layers, ending with tortillas. 5. When the layers of tortillas and fillings have just about reached the edge of the dish, add the remaining enchilada sauce and the remaining cheese to the top of the tortillas. 6. Cover the pan with foil. 7. Pour the water into the pot and place in the rack, and the place the pan on the rack. 8. Close the lid, turn the pressure release valve to SEAL position, and then move the slider to PRESSURE. Select HI and set the cooking time to 25 minutes. Press START/STOP to begin cooking. When finished, release the pressure quickly. 9. Take out the pan, remove the foil and let the dish sir for at least for 10 minutes before slicing. 10. Serve and enjoy.
**Per Serving:** Calories 743; Fat: 28.46g; Sodium: 1532mg; Carbs: 91.8g; Fibre: 6.3g; Sugar: 8.23g; Protein: 28.72g

## Easy Breads

**Prep Time:** 20 minutes | **Cook Time:** 5 minutes | **Serves:** 10

180 g plain flour
65 g whole wheat flour
1 tsp. salt
¼ tsp. garlic powder
180 ml hot water
2 tbsp. olive oil

1. Combine the flours, salt and garlic powder in a large bowl. Stir in water and oil. Turn onto a floured surface; knead them 10-12 times. 2. Divide dough into 10 portions, and then roll each portion into a 15 cm. circle on a lightly floured surface. 3. Add the breads to the pot. Move slider to AIR FRY/STOVETOP, and then use the dial to select SEAR/SAUTÉ. Select Lo3, and then press START/STOP to begin cooking. 4. Cook the breads for 1 minute on each side or until lightly browned. 5. Serve the breads warm.
**Per Serving:** Calories 113; Fat: 3.03g; Sodium: 234mg; Carbs: 18.68g; Fibre: 1.2g; Sugar: 0.08g; Protein: 2.74g

# Egg White Bites

**Prep Time:** 20 minutes | **Cook Time:** 25 minutes | **Serves:** 7 egg bites

15 g unsalted butter
½ yellow onion, sliced
Salt
Freshly ground black pepper
85 g thick-cut ham, diced
240 ml water
55 g shredded Swiss and Gruyère cheese blend
6 large egg whites
15 ml heavy cream
½ tsp. prepared ground horseradish
¼ tsp. dried thyme

1. Select SEAR/SAUTÉ. Select Lo3, and then press START/STOP to begin cooking. 2. Once the pot is hot, melt the butter. When the butter melts, add the onion, and sauté for about 10 minutes or until caramelized, then season them with salt and pepper. Stir in the diced ham and sauté for 5 more minutes. 3. Transfer the ham and caramelized onion to a plate to cool. Clean out the inside of the pot and return it to the device. Pour the water into the pot and insert the rack. 4. Place some caramelized onion and ham along with cheese in the bottom of each well of a silicone egg bite mold. 5. In a small bowl, whisk together the egg whites, cream, horseradish, salt, pepper and thyme. Pour the egg mixture over the ham mixture, filling each mold about three-quarters of the way full. 6. Carefully place the silicone egg bite mold on the rack. Close the lid, turn the pressure release valve to SEAL position, and then move the slider to PRESSURE. Select HI and set the cooking time to 8 minutes. Press START/STOP to begin cooking. When finished, release the pressure naturally. 7. Cut around the edges and release the egg bites from the mold. Flip the egg bites out onto a plate. Season them with more salt and pepper, if needed.

**Per Serving:** Calories 83; Fat: 4.53g; Sodium: 211mg; Carbs: 3.13g; Fibre: 0.2g; Sugar: 1.57g; Protein: 7.45g

## Crustless Mini Quiche Bites

**Prep Time:** 20 minutes | **Cook Time:** 10 minutes | **Serves:** 4

1 tsp. extra-virgin olive oil
5 large eggs
½ tsp. onion salt
½ tsp. dried basil
½ tsp. chopped fresh dill
½ tsp. chopped fresh parsley
75 g sliced cherry tomatoes
25 g chopped pitted green olives
75 g crumbled goat cheese
240 ml water

1. Place the olive oil on a paper towel and then use the paper towel to oil each well of the egg bite mold. 2. Whisk the eggs, onion salt, basil, dill and parsley in a medium bowl. 3. Add ¼ to ½ teaspoon each of the tomatoes, olives and goat cheese to the bottom of each well in the mold. Pour the egg mixture over the toppings to fill each well about three-quarters of the way up. Add the remaining tomatoes, olives and cheese on top of the egg mixture. 4. Pour the water in the pot and place in the rack, and then place the egg mold on the rack. 5. Close the lid, turn the pressure release valve to SEAL position, and then move the slider to PRESSURE. Select HI and set the cooking time to 8 minutes. Press START/STOP to begin cooking. When finished, release the pressure naturally. 6. Remove the egg bite mold. Flip the mini quiches out onto a serving dish. Enjoy.

**Per Serving:** Calories 191; Fat: 13.89g; Sodium: 192mg; Carbs: 1.35g; Fibre: 0.1g; Sugar: 0.83g; Protein: 14.61g

## Gruyère Crustless Quiche

**Prep Time:** 20 minutes | **Cook Time:** 35 minutes | **Serves:** 4

6 slices bacon
355 ml water
Nonstick cooking spray, for pan
6 large eggs
175 ml heavy cream
55 g shredded Gruyère cheese
1 tbsp chopped fresh parsley
½ tsp. coarse salt
Freshly ground black pepper

1. Select SEAR/SAUTÉ. Select Lo3, and then press START/STOP to begin cooking. 2. When the pot is hot, add the bacon and cook for about 5 minutes or until browned and crispy, and then transfer the bacon to paper towels to drain any excess fat. Discard the drippings without wiping clean. 3. Stop the process and scrape up any browned bits from the bottom of the pot. 4. Pour the water into the pot and place the rack in it. 5. Spray a suitable cake pan with nonstick cooking spray. 6. In a medium bowl, whisk together the eggs and cream until frothy. Crumble the bacon and stir it in along with the shredded cheese, parsley, salt and pepper. Pour the mixture into the prepared cake pan and place the pan on the rack. 7. Close the lid, turn the pressure release valve to SEAL position, and then move the slider to PRESSURE. Select HI and set the cooking time to 30 minutes. Press START/STOP to begin cooking. When finished, release the pressure quickly. 8. Carefully remove the cake pan from the pot. Slice the quiche and serve immediately.

**Per Serving:** Calories 390; Fat: 34.47g; Sodium: 706mg; Carbs: 2.04g; Fibre: 0g; Sugar: 1.59g; Protein: 17.56g

# Caramelised Vegetable Strata

**Prep Time:** 20 minutes | **Cook Time:** 30 minutes | **Serves:** 6-8

3 tbsp grass-fed butter or ghee, plus more for casserole
1 large yellow onion, thinly sliced
225 g cleaned white button or cremini mushrooms, thinly sliced
3 cloves garlic, finely chopped
1 tbsp. chopped fresh thyme
3 large eggs
240 ml milk
455 g loaf day-old gluten-free bread, cut into 2.5-cm cubes
115 g shredded sharp or mild cheddar cheese
40 g shredded Parmesan cheese
155 g frozen chopped spinach, thawed and moisture squeezed out
15 g chopped fresh flat-leaf parsley, plus more for garnish
Zest of 1 lemon
1 tsp. sea salt
355 ml water

1. Select SEAR/SAUTÉ. Select Lo3, and then press START/STOP to begin cooking. 2. When the pot is hot, melt the healthy fat you chose; add the onion and mushrooms, and cook them for 7 minutes until they are light golden brown and caramelised; add the garlic and thyme and cook them for 1 minute until fragrant. 3. Stop the process, and scrape up any browned bits at the bottom of the pot; transfer the onion mixture to a bowl and set aside. 4. Butter a suitable casserole dish and set aside. 5. In a huge bowl, whisk together the eggs and milk until fully incorporated. Add the bread cubes, shredded cheeses, onion mixture, spinach, parsley, lemon zest and salt, and then gently fold them to combine. 6. Pour the mixture into the prepared casserole dish and cover the dish with unbleached parchment paper, then top it with foil and secure it around the edges. 7. Pour the water into the pot and place in the rack, and then place the dish on the rack. 8. Close the lid, turn the pressure release valve to SEAL position, and then move the slider to PRESSURE. Select HI and set the cooking time to 30 minutes. Press START/STOP to begin cooking. When finished, release the pressure naturally. 9. Place the casserole dish on a baking sheet, and then place in the oven under a preheated broiler for about 3 minutes to crisp the top of the strata. Allow the dish to rest at room temperature for 10 minutes before serving.

**Per Serving:** Calories 280; Fat: 21.63g; Sodium: 573mg; Carbs: 8.66g; Fibre: 1.2g; Sugar: 2.99g; Protein: 13.54g

# Chapter 2 Soup, Chili and Stew

## Minestrone Soup

**Prep Time:** 10 minutes | **Cook Time:** 30 minutes | **Serves:** 4

320 g dried butter beans
230 g orzo
2 large carrots, peeled and diced
1 bunch Swiss chard, ribs removed and roughly chopped
1 medium courgette, diced
2 stalks celery, diced
1 medium onion, peeled and diced
1 teaspoon minced garlic
1 tablespoon Italian seasoning
1 teaspoon salt
½ teaspoon ground black pepper
2 bay leaves
1 can diced tomatoes, including juice
960 ml vegetable stock
240 ml tomato juice
4 sprigs fresh parsley for garnish

1. Rinse beans and add to the pot with remaining ingredients except parsley. 2. Close the lid, turn the pressure release valve to SEAL position, and then move the slider to PRESSURE. Select HI and set the cooking time to 30 minutes. Press START/STOP to begin cooking. When finished, release the pressure naturally. 3. Ladle the soup into bowls, garnish each bowl with a sprig of parsley, and serve warm.
**Per Serving:** Calories 581; Fat: 5.65g; Sodium: 2327mg; Carbs: 106.93g; Fibre: 27.9g; Sugar: 14.21g; Protein: 30.21g

## Sweet Potato & Wild Rice Chowder

**Prep Time:** 20 minutes | **Cook Time:** 45 minutes | **Serves:** 4

1 (455 g) bag frozen corn
1 large (300 g) sweet potato, peeled and chopped
1 medium yellow onion, chopped
2 celery ribs, chopped
100 g wild rice
1 teaspoon poultry seasoning
Salt and freshly ground black pepper

1. Combine the stock, corn, sweet potato, onion, celery, wild rice, and poultry seasoning in the pot. 2. Close the lid, turn the pressure release valve to SEAL position, and then move the slider to PRESSURE. Select HI and set the cooking time to 40 minutes. Press START/STOP to begin cooking. When finished, release the pressure naturally. 3. Select SEAR/SAUTÉ. Select Lo1, and then press START/STOP to begin cooking. Simmer the dish for 5 minutes more until bubbly and thickened slightly 4. Season the dish with salt and pepper and serve.
**Per Serving:** Calories 308; Fat: 2.08g; Sodium: 75mg; Carbs: 64.18g; Fibre: 8g; Sugar: 11.02g; Protein: 9.25g

## Mushroom Chicken Soup

**Prep Time:** 15 minutes | **Cook Time:** 25 minutes | **Serves:** 4

455 g chicken thighs cut in 1 cm cubes
1 teaspoon sea salt
½ teaspoon ground black pepper
2 tablespoons butter
1 small onion, peeled and diced
1 large carrot, peeled and diced
1 stalk celery, diced
200 g sliced mushrooms
960 ml chicken stock
2 teaspoons dried thyme
1 teaspoon dried oregano
1 teaspoon garlic powder
¼ teaspoon cayenne pepper
120 g heavy cream

1. Season the chicken thigh cubes with salt and pepper. Set aside. 2. Add the butter to the pot. Select SEAR/SAUTÉ. Select Lo3, and then press START/STOP to begin cooking. 3. When the butter melted, add the chicken, onion, carrot, celery, and mushrooms, and sauté them for 3 to 5 minutes until the onions are translucent. 4. Stop the process, and add the stock, thyme, oregano, garlic powder, and cayenne pepper. 5. Close the lid, turn the pressure release valve to SEAL position, and then move the slider to PRESSURE. Select HI and set the cooking time to 20 minutes. Press START/STOP to begin cooking. When finished, release the pressure quickly. 6. Stir in heavy cream. Ladle into bowls and serve warm.
**Per Serving:** Calories 517; Fat: 37.42g; Sodium: 2496mg; Carbs: 22.33g; Fibre: 1.2g; Sugar: 3.25g; Protein: 23.82g

## Chili Onion Mac

**Prep Time:** 25 minutes | **Cook Time:** 15 minutes | **Serves:** 4

1 tablespoon olive oil
455 g 95% lean beef mince
1 medium yellow onion, chopped
1 can crushed fire-roasted tomatoes
1 can kidney beans, drained
**Optional garnishes**
200 g grated cheddar
100 g elbow macaroni
240 ml store-bought beef stock
2 tablespoons plus 1½ teaspoons mild chili powder
Salt and freshly ground black pepper

240 g sour cream or homemade yogurt

1. Add the oil to the pot. Select SEAR/SAUTÉ. Select Lo3, and then press START/STOP to begin cooking. 2. When the oil is hot, add the beef and onions and cook them for 10 minutes until they begin to brown, leaving the beef in fairly large (2.5 cm) chunks for the best texture. 3. Stop the process, and add the tomatoes, beans, macaroni, stock, chili powder, ½ teaspoon salt, and several grinds of pepper to the pot. 4. Close the lid, turn the pressure release valve to SEAL position, and then move the slider to PRESSURE. Select HI and set the cooking time to 5 minutes. Press START/STOP to begin cooking. When finished, release the pressure naturally. 5. Season the dish with salt and pepper, or garnish the dish with the garnishes if desired. Enjoy.
**Per Serving:** Calories 495; Fat: 20.78g; Sodium: 434mg; Carbs: 38.83g; Fibre: 6.1g; Sugar: 7.32g; Protein: 38.2g

## Stuffed Potato Soup

**Prep Time:** 20 minutes | **Cook Time:** 10 minutes | **Serves:** 4

- 1 tablespoon safflower oil
- 1 large yellow onion, chopped
- 1.2 kg russet potatoes (3 large), peeled and cut into 2.5 – 3 cm chunks
- 600 ml store-bought chicken or vegetable stock
- Salt and freshly ground black pepper
- 120 g sour cream
- 150 g grated sharp cheddar cheese
- 4 slices thick-cut bacon, cooked and crumbled
- 4 green onions, thinly sliced

1. Select SEAR/SAUTÉ. Select Lo3, and then press START/STOP to begin cooking. 2. When the pot is hot, heat the oil, and then sauté the onion for 5 minutes until tender. 3. Stop the process, and add the potatoes, stock, and ¾ teaspoon salt to the pot. 4. Close the lid, turn the pressure release valve to SEAL position, and then move the slider to PRESSURE. Select HI and set the cooking time to 5 minutes. Press START/STOP to begin cooking. When finished, release the pressure quickly. 5. Remove the lid, add the sour cream and 75 g of the cheese, and stir gently with a rubber spatula until the cheese has melted and the largest chunks of potato are broken down into bite-size pieces. Season the dish with salt and pepper. 6. Serve garnished with the bacon, remaining cheese, and the green onions.

**Per Serving:** Calories 671; Fat: 36.17g; Sodium: 1176mg; Carbs: 64.77g; Fibre: 4.9g; Sugar: 4.37g; Protein: 24.03g

## Chili without Bean

**Prep Time:** 10 minutes | **Cook Time:** 40 minutes | **Serves:** 4

- 1 tablespoon olive oil
- 225 g pork mince
- 225 g beef mince
- 1 medium onion, peeled and diced
- 1 small green pepper, seeded and diced
- 1 large carrot, peeled and diced
- 3 cloves garlic, minced
- 2 tablespoons chili powder
- 1 teaspoon sea salt
- 2 teaspoons ground black pepper
- 1 small jalapeño, seeded and diced
- 1 can puréed tomatoes (including juice)

1. Add the oil to the pot. Select SEAR/SAUTÉ. Select Lo3, and then press START/STOP to begin cooking. 2. When the oil is hot, add the pork mince, beef mince, and onion, and sauté them for 5 minutes until the pork is no longer pink. 3. Stop the process and stir in the remaining ingredients. 4. Close the lid, turn the pressure release valve to SEAL position, and then move the slider to PRESSURE. Select HI and set the cooking time to 35 minutes. Press START/STOP to begin cooking. When finished, release the pressure naturally. 5. Serve warm.

**Per Serving:** Calories 422; Fat: 25.59g; Sodium: 1033mg; Carbs: 17.37g; Fibre: 7.1g; Sugar: 8.84g; Protein: 32.29g

## Pork Stew with Tomatoes & Pinto Bean

**Prep Time:** 20 minutes | **Cook Time:** 35 minutes | **Serves:** 6

455 g dried pinto beans, rinsed and drained
Salt and ground black pepper
½ teaspoon baking soda
1 teaspoon ground cumin
4 medium garlic cloves, thinly sliced
1 habanero chili, pierced a few times with a paring knife
1 tablespoon grated lime zest, plus 60 ml lime juice
2 tablespoons grated orange zest, plus 120 ml orange juice
700 g can diced fire-roasted tomatoes
3 tablespoons finely chopped coriander stems, plus 30 g lightly packed leaves, reserved separately
680 g boneless country-style pork ribs, trimmed and cut into 2.5 cm chunks
Sliced radishes, to serve

1. Stir together the beans, 2 teaspoons salt, the baking soda and 1.4 L water in the pot, then distribute in an even layer. 2. Close the lid, turn the pressure release valve to SEAL position, and then move the slider to PRESSURE. Select HI and set the cooking time to 5 minutes. Press START/STOP to begin cooking. When finished, release the pressure quickly. 3. Using potholders to carefully remove the pot from the unit and drain the beans in a colander; return the pot to the unit. 4. Rinse the beans under cool water and return to the pot. Stir in the cumin, garlic, habanero, lime zest and juice, orange zest and juice, the tomatoes with their juices, the coriander stems and the pork. Add 480 ml water; stir to combine, then distribute in an even layer. 5. Cook the dish at HI for 25 minutes on PRESSURE COOK mode, and release the pressure naturally. 6. Remove and discard the habanero. Let the dish stand for about 10 minutes, then taste and season with salt and pepper. Serve topped with the coriander leaves and sliced radishes.
**Per Serving:** Calories 491; Fat: 7.92g; Sodium: 358mg; Carbs: 63.44g; Fibre: 14.8g; Sugar: 12.43g; Protein: 41.65g

## Healthy Black Bean Soup

**Prep Time:** 15 minutes | **Cook Time:** 35 minutes | **Serves:** 6

1 tablespoon olive oil
2 stalks celery, chopped
1 medium yellow onion, peeled and chopped
2 cloves garlic, peeled and lightly crushed
½ teaspoon salt
10 g chopped fresh coriander
455 g dried black beans, soaked overnight in water to cover and drained
½ teaspoon dried thyme leaves
½ teaspoon ground cumin
960 ml vegetable stock
1 can diced tomatoes with green chilies, drained

1. Add the oil to the pot. Select SEAR/SAUTÉ. Select Lo3, and then press START/STOP to begin cooking. 2. When the oil is hot, add celery and onion, and cook them for 5 minutes until they are tender; add the garlic and salt, and cook them for 30 seconds until fragrant. 3. Stop the process, and add the coriander, beans, thyme, cumin, and stock to the pot. Close the lid, turn the pressure release valve to SEAL position, and then move the slider to PRESSURE. Select HI and set the cooking time to 30 minutes. Press START/STOP to begin cooking. When finished, release the pressure naturally. 4. Let the dish rest under KEEP WARM mode for 5 minutes before serving.
**Per Serving:** Calories 166; Fat: 5.3g; Sodium: 1330mg; Carbs: 25.76g; Fibre: 4.1g; Sugar: 4.16g; Protein: 5.67g

# Chili Texas

**Prep Time:** 30 minutes | **Cook Time:** 40 minutes | **Serves:** 4-6

| | |
|---|---|
| 1.2 kg boneless beef chuck, fat trimmed, cut into 2.5 cm – 3 cm chunks | 2 tablespoons chili powder |
| 1 tablespoon rapeseed oil | 1 large onion, chopped, 65 g set aside for garnish |
| Salt and freshly ground black pepper | 1 can fire-roasted diced tomatoes with green chilies, with juice |
| 70 g prepared mole paste (such as Doña Maria brand) | 2 tablespoons masa harina (corn flour) |
| 120 ml store-bought beef stock | |
| **Optional garnishes** | |
| 240 g sour cream | Sliced pickled jalapeños |

1. Toss the beef with oil in a foil-lined baking sheet; generously season the beef with salt and pepper, and then arrange them in an even layer. 2. Place the rack in the pot in the higher broil position and then place the sheet on it. Close the lid and move slider to AIR FRY/STOVETOP, then use the dial to select BROIL. Set the cooking time to 12 minutes and then press START/STOP to begin cooking. 3. Flip the beef halfway through. Transfer the beef and any accumulated juices to the pot. 4. Whisk together the mole paste, stock, and chili powder in a small bowl. 5. Add the stock mixture, onion, and tomatoes with juice to the pot and stir to combine. 6. Close the lid, turn the pressure release valve to SEAL position, and then move the slider to PRESSURE. Select HI and set the cooking time to 25 minutes. Press START/STOP to begin cooking. When finished, release the pressure naturally. 7. Place the masa harina in a small bowl and gradually whisk in 240 ml of the cooking liquid. Add the mixture to the chili and stir very gently. 8. Simmer them at Lo3 on SEAR/ SAUTÉ mode for 1 minute or until thickened and bubbly. 9. Season the chili with salt and pepper and serve with optional garnishes, if desired.

**Per Serving:** Calories 313; Fat: 13.62g; Sodium: 569mg; Carbs: 9.27g; Fibre: 1.4g; Sugar: 2.23g; Protein: 40.11g

## Cheese Squash Soup

**Prep Time:** 15 minutes | **Cook Time:** 20 minutes | **Serves:** 6

55 g unsalted butter
1 medium yellow onion, peeled and finely chopped
1 medium carrot, peeled and finely chopped
2 cloves garlic, peeled and minced
60 ml white wine
½ teaspoon dried thyme
⅛ teaspoon ground nutmeg
450 g cubed butternut squash
480 ml Vegetable Stock or Chicken Stock
2 tablespoons maple syrup
480 g heavy cream
100 g grated Emmental cheese
50 g grated sharp Cheddar cheese
3 tablespoons chopped fresh chives

1. Add the butter to the pot. Select SEAR/SAUTÉ. Select Lo3, and then press START/STOP to begin cooking. 2. When the butter melted, add the onion and carrot, and sauté them for 5 minutes; add the garlic and sauté for 30 seconds until fragrant; add wine and cook for 30 seconds until mostly evaporated, scraping the pot well. 3. Stop the process, and stir in the thyme, nutmeg, squash, and stock. 4. Close the lid, turn the pressure release valve to SEAL position, and then move the slider to PRESSURE. Select HI and set the cooking time to 15 minutes. Press START/STOP to begin cooking. When finished, release the pressure naturally. 5. Remove lid and stir in maple syrup. Use an immersion blender to purée soup until smooth. 6. Stir cream into soup, then whisk in both grated cheeses 25 g at a time, adding more cheese once the previous addition is fully melted. Let stand on the Keep Warm setting for 5 minutes. 7. Serve the dish hot with chives for garnish.

**Per Serving:** Calories 422; Fat: 32.78g; Sodium: 398mg; Carbs: 22.23g; Fibre: 2.6g; Sugar: 10.12g; Protein: 12.21g

## Sausage & Bean Soup

**Prep Time:** 10 minutes | **Cook Time:** 10 minutes | **Serves:** 6

2 tablespoons olive oil
2 stalks celery, chopped
1 medium carrot, peeled and chopped
1 medium yellow onion, peeled and chopped
2 cloves garlic, peeled and lightly crushed
½ teaspoon salt
455 g smoked beef sausage, cut into 1 cm slices
2 cans black beans, drained and rinsed
½ teaspoon dried thyme leaves
¼ teaspoon dried oregano leaves
960 ml chicken stock

1. Add the oil to the pot. Select SEAR/SAUTÉ. Select Lo3, and then press START/STOP to begin cooking. 2. When the oil is hot, add the celery, carrot, and onion, and cook them for 5 minutes until they are tender; add the garlic and salt, and cook them for 30 seconds until fragrant. 3. Stop the process, and add the sausage, beans, thyme, oregano, and stock to the pot. 4. Close the lid, turn the pressure release valve to SEAL position, and then move the slider to PRESSURE. Select HI and set the cooking time to 8 minutes. Press START/STOP to begin cooking. When finished, release the pressure naturally. 5. Stir the dish well and serve hot.

**Per Serving:** Calories 279; Fat: 19.08g; Sodium: 1495mg; Carbs: 15.57g; Fibre: 4.7g; Sugar: 2.81g; Protein: 16.55g

## Cheese Macaroni Soup

**Prep Time:** 15 minutes | **Cook Time:** 10 minutes | **Serves:** 8

- 3 tablespoons unsalted butter
- 2 medium carrots, peeled and finely chopped
- 2 stalks celery, diced
- 1 medium onion, peeled and diced
- 1 clove garlic, minced
- 1 teaspoon dried mustard
- 720 ml chicken stock
- 200 g elbow macaroni
- 240 g heavy cream
- 200 g shredded sharp Cheddar cheese
- 100 g shredded American cheese

1. Add the butter to the pot. Select SEAR/SAUTÉ. Select Lo3, and then press START/STOP to begin cooking. 2. When the butter melted, add carrots, celery, and onion, and cook them for 5 minutes until softened; add garlic and cook them for 30 seconds until fragrant, then add mustard and stir them well. 3. Stop the process and pour in the stock. 4. Close the lid, turn the pressure release valve to SEAL position, and then move the slider to PRESSURE. Select HI and set the cooking time to 5 minutes. Press START/STOP to begin cooking. When finished, release the pressure naturally. 5. Open lid and stir soup well. Stir in cream, and then stir in cheese 100 g at a time, stirring each addition until completely melted before adding another. 6. Serve hot.

**Per Serving:** Calories 540; Fat: 30.26g; Sodium: 990mg; Carbs: 29g; Fibre: 1.7g; Sugar: 4.81g; Protein: 36.61g

## Beef Reuben Soup

**Prep Time:** 20 minutes | **Cook Time:** 20 minutes | **Serves:** 6

- 1 tablespoon unsalted butter
- 1 medium yellow onion, peeled and chopped
- 3 cloves garlic, peeled and minced
- ¼ teaspoon ground fennel
- ¼ teaspoon salt
- ¼ teaspoon ground black pepper
- 2 tablespoons plain flour
- 720 ml beef stock
- 1 medium russet potato, peeled and chopped
- 455 g cooked corned beef, chopped
- 140 g drained sauerkraut
- 60 g heavy cream
- 75 g grated Swiss cheese
- 2 spring onions, chopped

1. Add the butter to the pot. Select SEAR/SAUTÉ. Select Lo3, and then press START/STOP to begin cooking. 2. When the butter melted, add onion and cook them for 5 minutes until tender; add garlic, fennel, salt, and pepper, and cook them for 30 seconds until fragrant; add flour and cook for 1 minute, making sure flour coats the onions; stir in the stock, making sure to scrape any bits off the bottom of pot; mix in the potato, corned beef, and sauerkraut. 3. Stop the process. 4. Close the lid, turn the pressure release valve to SEAL position, and then move the slider to PRESSURE. Select HI and set the cooking time to 20 minutes. Press START/STOP to begin cooking. When finished, release the pressure quickly. 5. Open the lid and stir soup well. Add cream and cheese and stir until cheese is completely melted. 6. Serve the dish hot with spring onions for garnish.

**Per Serving:** Calories 313; Fat: 14.54g; Sodium: 780mg; Carbs: 17.98g; Fibre: 2.1g; Sugar: 2.17g; Protein: 28.38g

# Enchilada Chicken Soup

**Prep Time:** 25 minutes | **Cook Time:** 30 minutes | **Serves:** 6

| | |
|---|---|
| 1 tablespoon vegetable oil | ¼ teaspoon salt |
| 1 medium yellow onion, peeled and chopped | ¼ teaspoon ground black pepper |
| 10 g chopped fresh coriander | 720 ml chicken stock |
| 3 cloves garlic, peeled and minced | 2 (150 g) boneless, skinless chicken breasts |
| 1 small jalapeño pepper, seeded and minced | 60 g water |
| 1 (250 g) can diced green tomatoes with green chilies, drained | 3 tablespoons masa |
| | 100 g grated sharp Cheddar cheese |
| ½ teaspoon ground cumin | 120 g sour cream |
| ¼ teaspoon ground coriander | 75 g tortilla chips |

1. Add the oil to the pot. Select SEAR/SAUTÉ. Select Lo3, and then press START/STOP to begin cooking. 2. When the oil is hot, add onion and cook them for 5 minutes until tender; add coriander, garlic, jalapeño, tomatoes, cumin, coriander, salt, and pepper, and cook them for 1 minute until fragrant. 3. Stop the process, and stir in the stock and chicken. 4. Close the lid, turn the pressure release valve to SEAL position, and then move the slider to PRESSURE. Select HI and set the cooking time to 20 minutes. Press START/STOP to begin cooking. When finished, release the pressure naturally. 5. Open lid and transfer chicken to a cutting board. Shred meat with two forks and set aside. 6. In a small bowl, combine water and masa, then whisk into soup. 7. Select the SEAR/SAUTÉ mode and cook them for 8 minutes until the soup has thickened, stirring constantly. 8. Once soup stops bubbling, stir in chicken, cheese, and sour cream and stir until the cheese is completely melted. 9. Serve the soup hot with tortilla chips for garnish.

**Per Serving:** Calories 451; Fat: 22.96g; Sodium: 1212mg; Carbs: 23.53g; Fibre: 2g; Sugar: 7.21g; Protein: 36.67g

## Spicy Chicken

**Prep Time:** 15 minutes | **Cook Time:** 40 minutes | **Serves:** 8

- 1 tablespoon olive oil
- 455 g chicken mince
- 1 medium yellow onion, peeled and diced
- 3 cloves garlic, minced
- 3 canned chipotle chilies in adobo sauce
- 1 can dark red kidney beans, drained and rinsed
- 1 can black beans, drained and rinsed
- 1 teaspoon Worcestershire sauce
- 1 can diced tomatoes, including liquid
- 1 can diced green chilies, including liquid
- 1 teaspoon sea salt
- 2 teaspoons hot sauce
- 1 teaspoon smoked paprika
- 1 teaspoon chili powder

1. Add the oil to the pot. Select SEAR/SAUTÉ. Select Lo3, and then press START/STOP to begin cooking. 2. When the oil is hot, add the chicken mince and onion, and sauté them for 5 minutes until chicken is no longer pink. 3. Stir in the remaining ingredients and stop the process. 4. Close the lid, turn the pressure release valve to SEAL position, and then move the slider to PRESSURE. Select HI and set the cooking time to 35 minutes. Press START/STOP to begin cooking. When finished, release the pressure naturally. 5. Ladle the dish into individual bowls and serve warm.
**Per Serving:** Calories 272; Fat: 12.3g; Sodium: 1472mg; Carbs: 27.06g; Fibre: 11g; Sugar: 9.43g; Protein: 17.87g

## Vegetables & Chicken Breasts

**Prep Time:** 25 minutes | **Cook Time:** 15 minutes | **Serves:** 4

- 1 tablespoon olive oil
- 1 medium yellow onion, chopped
- 2 medium carrots, chopped
- 2 celery ribs, sliced
- 455 g boneless, skinless chicken breasts
- Salt and freshly ground black pepper
- 720 ml store-bought chicken stock
- 240 ml Bisquick
- 80 ml milk

1. Season the chicken breasts all over with salt and pepper. 2. Add the oil to the pot. Select SEAR/SAUTÉ. Select Lo3, and then press START/STOP to begin cooking. 3. When the oil is hot, add onion, carrot, and celery, and cook them for 4 minutes until tender. 4. Add the chicken and stock to the pot, and stop the process. 5. Close the lid, turn the pressure release valve to SEAL position, and then move the slider to PRESSURE. Select HI and set the cooking time to 5 minutes. Press START/STOP to begin cooking. When finished, release the pressure quickly. 6. Transfer the chicken to a clean cutting board and chop into bite-size pieces. Return the chicken pieces to the pot. 7. In a medium bowl, mix the Bisquick with the milk until the mixture comes together into a sticky batter. 8. Drop the batter by tablespoons into the pot. Cover with a regular pan lid that fits snugly on top. 9. Select SEAR/SAUTÉ mode, and cook the dumplings at Lo3 for 5 minutes until they are fluffy and cooked through. 10. Serve the dish immediately.
**Per Serving:** Calories 280; Fat: 11.19g; Sodium: 1037mg; Carbs: 31.81g; Fibre: 3.2g; Sugar: 10.92g; Protein: 13.06g

## Beef mince Stew

**Prep Time:** 25 minutes | **Cook Time:** 25 minutes | **Serves:** 6

1 tablespoon solid or liquid fat of your choice
675 g lean beef mince
240 ml stock of your choice
2 tablespoons tomato paste
800 g chopped quick-cooking vegetables
2 tablespoons vinegar
Up to 1½ tablespoons dried herbs and/or spices
1 tablespoon soy sauce
1 teaspoon ground black pepper
Up to 1 teaspoon red pepper flakes (optional)
100 – 200 g shredded semi-firm cheese

1. Add the oil to the pot. Select SEAR/SAUTÉ. Select Lo3, and then press START/STOP to begin cooking. 2. When the oil is hot, add the beef mince and cook them for 2 to 3 minutes until the meat loses its raw, pink color, breaking up any clumps; pour in the stock and add the tomato paste, and then stir them until the paste has dissolved. 3. Stop the process, and stir in the quick-cooking vegetables, vinegar, dried herb and/or spice blend, soy sauce, black pepper, and red pepper flakes (optional). 4. Close the lid, turn the pressure release valve to SEAL position, and then move the slider to PRESSURE. Select HI and set the cooking time to 5 minutes. Press START/STOP to begin cooking. When finished, release the pressure quickly. 5. Unlatch the lid and open the cooker. Stir in the cheese, and then set the lid askew over the pot for 5 minutes to melt the cheese and blend the flavors. 6. Stir the dish again before serving.
**Per Serving:** Calories 462; Fat: 21.63g; Sodium: 769mg; Carbs: 24.12g; Fibre: 7.4g; Sugar: 7.85g; Protein: 40.45g

## Lamb Stew in Beef Stock

**Prep Time:** 15 minutes | **Cook Time:** 40 minutes | **Serves:** 6

2 tablespoons olive oil
900 g cubed boneless lamb
1 medium onion, peeled and diced
4 garlic cloves, minced
60 ml freshly squeezed orange juice
480 ml beef stock
150 g crushed tomatoes
45 g diced pitted dates
45 g diced dried apricots
2 teaspoons ground cumin
¼ teaspoon ground cinnamon
¼ teaspoon cayenne pepper
2 teaspoons minced fresh ginger
1 teaspoon sea salt
½ teaspoon ground black pepper
20 g chopped fresh coriander

1. Add the oil to the pot. Select SEAR/SAUTÉ. Select Lo3, and then press START/STOP to begin cooking. 2. When the oil is hot, add the lamb cubes and onion, and cook them for 3 to 5 minutes until the onions are translucent; add the garlic and sauté them for 1 minute. 3. Add orange juice and beef stock to the pot and deglaze by scraping any of the bits from the side of the pot. Stir in the remaining ingredients (except coriander ). 4. Close the lid, turn the pressure release valve to SEAL position, and then move the slider to PRESSURE. Select HI and set the cooking time to 35 minutes. Press START/STOP to begin cooking. When finished, release the pressure naturally. 5. Ladle the dish into individual bowls, garnish with coriander, and serve warm.
**Per Serving:** Calories 343; Fat: 16.66g; Sodium: 719mg; Carbs: 15.16g; Fibre: 2.3g; Sugar: 10.16g; Protein: 33.12g

## Loaded Bacon Potato Soup

**Prep Time:** 10 minutes | **Cook Time:** 30 minutes | **Serves:** 4

- 2 slices bacon, diced
- 4 tablespoons butter
- 1 medium sweet onion, peeled and chopped
- 1 large carrot, peeled and diced
- 2 cloves garlic, chopped
- 600 g peeled and diced potatoes
- 960 ml chicken stock
- 1 teaspoon sea salt
- 1 teaspoon ground black pepper
- Pinch of ground nutmeg
- 240 ml whole milk

1. Select SEAR/SAUTÉ. Select Lo3, and then press START/STOP to begin cooking. 2. Add the bacon to the pot and stir-fry the bacon until almost crisp; add the butter, onion, and carrot, and sauté them for 3 to 5 minutes until the onions are translucent; add garlic and sauté for an additional minute; add potatoes and continue to sauté for 2 to 3 minutes until potatoes are browned. 3. Stir in the stock, salt, pepper, and nutmeg, and stop the process. 4. Close the lid, turn the pressure release valve to SEAL position, and then move the slider to PRESSURE. Select HI and set the cooking time to 20 minutes. Press START/STOP to begin cooking. When finished, release the pressure naturally. 5. Add the milk to the pot, and then purée the soup with an immersion blender in it. 6. Ladle the soup into bowls and serve warm.

**Per Serving:** Calories 742; Fat: 35.38g; Sodium: 1777mg; Carbs: 44.97g; Fibre: 4.8g; Sugar: 14.14g; Protein: 59.46g

## Simple Firehouse Chili

**Prep Time:** 20 minutes | **Cook Time:** 15 minutes | **Serves:** 6

- 2 tablespoons olive, vegetable, corn, or rapeseed oil
- 2 medium green peppers, stemmed, cored, and chopped
- 1 medium yellow onion, chopped
- 2 medium garlic cloves, peeled and minced
- 900 g plum or Roma tomatoes, chopped
- 25 g standard chili powder
- 1 tablespoon dried oregano
- 2 teaspoons ground cumin
- 1 teaspoon ground coriander
- 1 teaspoon table salt
- 1 can red kidney beans, drained and rinsed
- 180 ml chicken stock
- 900 g lean beef mince
- 60 g tomato paste

1. Add the oil to the pot. Select SEAR/SAUTÉ. Select Lo3, and then press START/STOP to begin cooking. 2. When the oil is hot, add pepper , onion, and garlic, and cook them for 5 minutes until the onion softens; stir in the tomatoes and cook them for 2 minutes until they begin to soften; stir in the chili powder, oregano, cumin, coriander, and salt, and cook them for a few seconds until fragrant. 3. Stop the process, then add the beans and stock , and crumble in the beef mince. 4. Close the lid, turn the pressure release valve to SEAL position, and then move the slider to PRESSURE. Select HI and set the cooking time to 6 minutes. Press START/STOP to begin cooking. When finished, release the pressure naturally. 5. Unlatch the lid, and stir in the tomato paste, then simmer them at Lo3 on SEAR/SAUTÉ mode for 2 to 3 minutes until a little bit thickened and almost irresistible. 6. Serve warm.

**Per Serving:** Calories 598; Fat: 19.92g; Sodium: 747mg; Carbs: 52.99g; Fibre: 6.7g; Sugar: 38.59g; Protein: 52.33g

# Chapter 3 Vegetables and Sides

## Barbecue Tofu Sandwiches

**Prep Time:** 20 minutes | **Cook Time:** 15 minutes | **Serves:** 6

| | |
|---|---|
| 1 tablespoon olive oil | Freshly ground black pepper |
| 1 medium yellow onion, sliced through root end | 455 g extra-firm tofu, patted dry and cut into 1 x 5 cm sticks |
| 1 red pepper , thinly sliced | 4 hamburger buns, toasted |
| 160 g thick barbecue sauce | |
| 2 tablespoons balsamic or red wine vinegar | |

1. Add the oil to the pot. Select SEAR/SAUTÉ. Select Lo3, and then press START/STOP to begin cooking. 2. When the oil is hot, add onion and pepper , and cook them for 4 minutes until they begin to brown. 3. Stop the process, and stir in barbecue sauce, 60 ml water, the vinegar, and several grinds of pepper, then add the tofu and stir them gently. 4. Close the lid, turn the pressure release valve to SEAL position, and then move the slider to PRESSURE. Select HI and set the cooking time to 3 minutes. Press START/STOP to begin cooking. When finished, release the pressure quickly. 5. Transfer the tofu and vegetables to a large bowl; cover the bowl with foil. 6. Simmer the left food in the pot at Hi5 on SEAR/SAUTÉ mode for 3 minutes until the sauce has thickened. 7. Mound the tofu and veggies on the bottom half of the buns. Drizzle with some of the sauce and sandwich with the bun tops. Serve immediately.

**Per Serving:** Calories 141; Fat: 7.18g; Sodium: 73mg; Carbs: 12.21g; Fibre: 1g; Sugar: 4.21g; Protein: 8.98g

## Broccoli with Garlic Dressing

**Prep Time:** 15 minutes | **Cook Time:** 5 minutes | **Serves:** 4

| | |
|---|---|
| 4 medium garlic cloves, unpeeled, left whole | 1 teaspoon Dijon mustard |
| 455 g broccoli, cut into 2.5 – 3 cm florets, stems thinly sliced | 60 ml olive oil |
| 2 tablespoons fresh lemon juice | Salt and freshly ground black pepper |

1. Place 240 ml warm water and the garlic in the pot. Set the Cook & Crisp Basket in the pot and place the broccoli in it. 2. Close the lid, turn the pressure release valve to SEAL position, and then move the slider to PRESSURE. Select HI and set the cooking time to 1 minute. Press START/STOP to begin cooking. When finished, release the pressure quickly. 3. Transfer the broccoli to a large serving bowl. Remove the basket from the pot. 4. Transfer the garlic to a cutting board, discard the peels, and chop the cloves. In a medium bowl, combine the garlic, lemon juice, and mustard. Gradually whisk in the oil. 5. Toss the broccoli with the dressing and season with salt and pepper.

**Per Serving:** Calories 151; Fat: 14.13g; Sodium: 52mg; Carbs: 4.84g; Fibre: 3.2g; Sugar: 0.66g; Protein: 3.86g

## Middle Eastern Lentils & Rice

**Prep Time:** 25 minutes | **Cook Time:** 20 minutes | **Serves:** 4-6

190 g dark green lentils du Puy
960 ml boiling water
2 tablespoons olive oil
1 large yellow onion, thinly sliced
3 medium garlic cloves, finely chopped
1¼ teaspoons ground cumin
720 ml store-bought vegetable stock, or water
Salt and freshly ground black pepper
200 g basmati rice, rinsed and drained
240 g plain Greek yogurt or 4 fried eggs

1. Pour the lentils into a large bowl and add the boiling water; set aside. 2. Add the oil to the pot. Select SEAR/SAUTÉ. Select Hi5, and then press START/STOP to begin cooking. 3. When the oil is hot, add the onion and sauté them for 10 to 12 minutes until they are well browned; add 60 ml water and simmer for 30 seconds until evaporated, scraping up any browned bits from the bottom of the pot; add the garlic and cumin, ad cook them for 30 seconds until fragrant. 4. Stop the process and set aside 30 g of the onion mixture for garnish. 5. Drain the lentils and add them to the pot with the onion. Add 480 ml of the stock, 1¼ teaspoons salt, and several grinds of pepper. Place the rack in the pot. 6. Combine the rice, the remaining 240 ml stock, and a generous pinch of salt in a suitable baking pan. 7. Place the baking pan on the rack. 8. Close the lid, turn the pressure release valve to SEAL position, and then move the slider to PRESSURE. Select HI and set the cooking time to 4 minutes. Press START/STOP to begin cooking. When finished, release the pressure naturally. 9. Fluff the rice with a fork. Remove the rack and gently stir the lentils and rice together. Garnish the dish with the reserved fried onions and serve with yogurt or fried eggs.

**Per Serving:** Calories 156; Fat: 9.61g; Sodium: 138mg; Carbs: 16.57g; Fibre: 5.1g; Sugar: 2.89g; Protein: 7.51g

## Flamboyant Flamenco Salad

**Prep Time:** 25 minutes | **Cook Time:** 0 minute | **Serves:** 8

3 medium rainbow carrots
4 medium blood oranges, peeled and segmented
½ small red onion, thinly sliced
½ medium fresh beetroot, thinly sliced
½ medium watermelon radish, thinly sliced
2 radishes, thinly sliced
2 tbsp. chopped pistachios, toasted
2 tbsp. chopped oil-packed sun-dried tomatoes
1 tbsp. capers, drained
¼ tsp. salt
¼ tsp. pepper
60 ml white balsamic vinaigrette
120 g torn leaf lettuce
25 g shaved Manchego or Parmesan cheese

1. Using a vegetable peeler, shave carrots lengthwise into very thin slices; place them in a large bowl. 2. Add oranges, red onion, beet, radishes, pistachios, tomatoes, capers, salt and pepper. Drizzle them with dressing; lightly toss to coat. 3. Arrange lettuce on a platter; top the salad with vegetable mixture and top with cheese. Enjoy.

**Per Serving:** Calories 72; Fat: 1.22g; Sodium: 150mg; Carbs: 14.24g; Fibre: 2.9g; Sugar: 8.16g; Protein: 2.6g

## Japanese-Style Vegetable Curry

**Prep Time:** 15 minutes | **Cook Time:** 15 minutes | **Serves:** 4

1 tablespoon rapeseed oil
1 large onion, sliced through the root end
4 cubes mild Japanese curry sauce mix
455 g winter squash or Yukon Gold potatoes, peeled and cut into 2.5 cm chunks
2 large carrots, peeled and cut at an angle into 2.5 cm -thick slices
455 g extra-firm tofu, cut into 2.5 cm cubes
Cooked udon noodles or steamed rice, for serving

1. Add the oil to the pot. Select SEAR/SAUTÉ. Select Hi5, and then press START/STOP to begin cooking. 2. When the oil is hot, add the onions and cook them for 4 minutes until they are tender. 3. Stop the process, add the curry mix and 360 ml water to the pot, and break up the curry cubes; add the squash and carrots and stir them very gently to combine; place the tofu cubes on top, but do not stir them in. 4. Close the lid, turn the pressure release valve to SEAL position, and then move the slider to PRESSURE. Select HI and set the cooking time to 8 minutes. Press START/STOP to begin cooking. When finished, release the pressure quickly. 5. Stir the dish gently to combine the tofu and other ingredients without breaking up the tofu. 6. Serve the dish with hot noodles or rice.
**Per Serving:** Calories 305; Fat: 12.95g; Sodium: 477mg; Carbs: 36.87g; Fibre: 3.4g; Sugar: 3.7g; Protein: 14.43g

## Crispy Parmesan Polenta

**Prep Time:** 10 minutes | **Cook Time:** 25 minutes | **Serves:** 4

2 tablespoons olive oil
2 medium garlic cloves, thinly sliced
960 ml store-bought chicken or vegetable stock , warmed
1 bay leaf
Salt and freshly ground black pepper
125 g polenta (not quick-cooking)
50 g grated Parmesan cheese

1. Add the oil to the pot. Select SEAR/SAUTÉ. Select Lo3, and then press START/STOP to begin cooking. 2. When the oil is hot, add the garlic and cook for 30 seconds; add the stock , bay leaf, and ½ teaspoon salt, and when the liquid comes to simmer, gradually whisk in the polenta. 3. Stop the process. 4. Close the lid, turn the pressure release valve to SEAL position, and then move the slider to PRESSURE. Select LO and set the cooking time to 9 minutes. Press START/STOP to begin cooking. When finished, release the pressure naturally. 5. Unlock the lid. It will look watery at first, but will come together and thicken as it stands. Whisk in the cheese and season with salt and pepper. Discard the bay leaf before serving. 6. For solid polenta to pan-fry, transfer the polenta to a storage container without lid and refrigerate them for at least 2 hours until solid. 7. Cut into squares and pan-fry in a nonstick sauté pan with a few tablespoons of olive oil over medium heat for 5 minutes on each side or until golden brown. 8. Serve warm.
**Per Serving:** Calories 296; Fat: 17.32g; Sodium: 814mg; Carbs: 25.78g; Fibre: 3.8g; Sugar: 7.01g; Protein: 10.62g

# Cannellini Beans with Tomatoes

**Prep Time:** 20 minutes | **Cook Time:** 30 minutes | **Serves:** 4-6

455 g dried cannellini beans (see note), rinsed and drained
Salt and ground black pepper
½ teaspoon baking soda
3 tablespoons extra-virgin olive oil, plus more to serve
1 medium yellow onion, chopped
4 medium garlic cloves, thinly sliced
1 tablespoon fennel seeds
½ teaspoon red pepper flakes
360g can diced tomatoes
1 piece Parmesan cheese rind (optional), plus shaved Parmesan to serve
20 g lightly packed fresh basil, torn

1. Stir the beans, 2 teaspoons salt, the baking soda and 1.4 L water in the pot, then distribute in an even layer. 2. Close the lid, turn the pressure release valve to SEAL position, and then move the slider to PRESSURE. Select HI and set the cooking time to 5 minutes. Press START/STOP to begin cooking. When finished, release the pressure quickly. 3. Carefully remove the pot from the unit and drain the beans in a colander; return the pot to the unit. Rinse the beans under cool water, set aside. 4. Add the oil to the pot. Select SEAR/SAUTÉ. Select Lo3, and then press START/STOP to begin cooking. 5. When the oil is shimmering, add onion, garlic, fennel seeds, pepper flakes and 1 teaspoon salt, and cook them for 3 minutes until the onion begins to soften; add the tomatoes with the juices and cook them for 6 to 7 minutes until the liquid has almost evaporated; add the beans and Parmesan rind (optional), then stir in 720 ml water; distribute in an even layer. 6. Close the lid, turn the pressure release valve to SEAL position, and then move the slider to PRESSURE. Select HI and set the cooking time to 16 minutes. Press START/STOP to begin cooking. When finished, release the pressure naturally. 7. Let the dish stand for about 15 minutes, then remove and discard the Parmesan rind (if used). Taste and season the dish with salt and pepper, then stir in half of the basil. 8. Serve topped with the remaining basil, shaved Parmesan, black pepper and additional oil.

**Per Serving:** Calories 49; Fat: 0.74g; Sodium: 424mg; Carbs: 10.24g; Fibre: 3.8g; Sugar: 4.07g; Protein: 2.3g

# Spiced Kidney Bean Stew

**Prep Time:** 25 minutes | **Cook Time:** 30 minutes | **Serves:** 4-6

455 g dried red kidney beans, rinsed and drained
Salt and ground black pepper
½ teaspoon baking soda
3 tablespoons extra-virgin olive oil
1 large yellow onion, halved and thinly sliced
6 medium garlic cloves, finely chopped
3 tablespoons finely grated fresh ginger
2 tablespoons garam masala
1 tablespoon ground cumin
2 teaspoons curry powder
700 g can whole peeled tomatoes, drained, 240 ml juices reserved, tomatoes crushed by hand
20 g finely chopped fresh coriander

1. Stir the beans, 2 teaspoons salt, the baking soda and 1.4 L water in the pot. 2. Close the lid, turn the pressure release valve to SEAL position, and then move the slider to PRESSURE. Select HI and set the cooking time to 5 minutes. Press START/STOP to begin cooking. When finished, release the pressure naturally. 3. Carefully remove the pot from the unit and drain the beans in a colander; return the pot to the unit. Rinse the beans under cool water; set aside. 4. Add the oil to the pot. Select SEAR/SAUTÉ. Select Lo3, and then press START/STOP to begin cooking. 5. When the oil is hot, add the garlic, ginger, garam masala, cumin and curry powder, and cook them for 30 seconds until fragrant; stir in the tomatoes and reserved juices, scraping up any browned bits; stir in 720 ml water, the beans and 1½ teaspoons salt, then distribute in an even layer. 6. Close the lid, turn the pressure release valve to SEAL position, and then move the slider to PRESSURE. Select HI and set the cooking time to 15 minutes. Press START/STOP to begin cooking. When finished, release the pressure naturally. 7. Stir the beans, and cook the food at Hi5 on SEAR/SAUTÉ mode for 5 to 8 minutes. 8. Let the dish stand for 10 minutes, then stir in the coriander . Taste and season the dish with salt and pepper.

**Per Serving:** Calories 161; Fat: 4.12g; Sodium: 447mg; Carbs: 25.84g; Fibre: 9.3g; Sugar: 6.92g; Protein: 7.61g

# Red Lentil and Bulgur Soup

**Prep Time:** 15 minutes | **Cook Time:** 20 minutes | **Serves:** 4

- 180 g plain whole-milk yogurt
- 2 teaspoons grated lemon zest, plus lemon wedges to serve
- 30 g lightly packed fresh mint leaves, finely chopped, divided
- Salt and ground black pepper
- 6 tablespoons salted butter, cut into 1 tablespoon-pieces, divided
- 285 g red lentils, rinsed and drained
- 50 g coarse bulgur
- 1 large yellow onion, finely chopped
- 2 medium garlic cloves, finely chopped
- 3 tablespoons tomato paste
- 2 tablespoons harissa, plus more to serve
- 2 tablespoons sweet paprika

1. In a small bowl, stir together the yogurt, lemon zest, half the mint and ¼ teaspoon each salt and pepper. Cover the bowl and refrigerate the mixture until ready to serve. 2. Select SEAR/SAUTÉ. Select Lo3, and then press START/STOP to begin cooking. 3. Add 3 tablespoons of butter and cook for 1 to 2 minutes until it begins to smell nutty and the milk solids at the bottom begin to brown. 4. Stop the process, and carefully remove the pot from the unit and pour the browned butter into a small microwave-safe bowl, scraping out the butter with a silicone spatula. 5. Return the pot to the unit, then add the remaining 2 tablespoons butter, the lentils, bulgur, onion, garlic, tomato paste, harissa, paprika and 2 teaspoons salt. Stir them, then pour in 1.7 L water and distribute the mixture in an even layer. 6. Close the lid, turn the pressure release valve to SEAL position, and then move the slider to PRESSURE. Select HI and set the cooking time to 15 minutes. Press START/STOP to begin cooking. When finished, release the pressure naturally. 7. Stir the soup, scraping the bottom of the pot, then stir in the remaining mint. Taste and season the dish with salt. If the browned butter has solidified, microwave on high for 10 to 15 seconds until melted. 8. Ladle the soup into bowls, drizzle with browned butter and dollop with the yogurt mixture, then sprinkle with additional pepper. Offer lemon wedges and additional harissa on the side.

**Per Serving:** Calories 471; Fat: 17.86g; Sodium: 202mg; Carbs: 61.13g; Fibre: 10.8g; Sugar: 7.97g; Protein: 21.31g

# Curried Chickpeas with Coriander

**Prep Time:** 35 minutes | **Cook Time:** 40 minutes | **Serves:** 4-6

455 g dried chickpeas, rinsed and drained
Salt and ground black pepper
½ teaspoon baking soda
10 cm piece fresh ginger, peeled and cut into 4 pieces
1 serrano chili, stemmed, halved and seeded
6 medium garlic cloves, smashed and peeled
1 tablespoon ground coriander
1 tablespoon ground cumin
1 bunch coriander, stems and leaves roughly chopped
4 spring onions, roughly chopped
3 tablespoons coconut oil
3 tablespoons lime juice, plus lime wedges to serve
Whole-milk yogurt, to serve

1. Mix together the chickpeas, 2 teaspoons salt, the baking soda and 1.4 L water in the pot, then distribute in an even layer. 2. Close the lid, turn the pressure release valve to SEAL position, and then move the slider to PRESSURE. Select HI and set the cooking time to 5 minutes. Press START/STOP to begin cooking. When finished, release the pressure naturally. 3. Drain the chickpeas in a colander; return the pot to the unit. Rinse the chickpeas under cool water; set aside. 4. In a food processor, combine the ginger, chili, garlic, coriander and cumin; process them for 1 minute until finely chopped, scraping the bowl as needed. Transfer the mixture to a small bowl. 5. Add the coriander, spring onions and 120 ml water to the now-empty food processor, and then process them for 30 seconds until smooth. Transfer the mixture to another small bowl, press plastic wrap directly against the surface and refrigerate until ready to use. 6. Select SEAR/SAUTÉ. Select Lo3, and then press START/STOP to begin cooking. 7. Add the coconut oil and let melt, then add the chili mixture and cook for 1 minute until fragrant. Add the chickpeas, 1½ teaspoons salt and 960 ml water; stir them to combine, and then distribute them in an even layer. 8. Close the lid, turn the pressure release valve to SEAL position, and then move the slider to PRESSURE. Select HI and set the cooking time to 20 minutes. Press START/STOP to begin cooking. When finished, release the pressure naturally. 9. Stir the chickpeas and cook them at Hi5 for 8 to 10 minutes until the liquid is slightly thickened. 10. Carefully remove the pot from the unit and let the dish stand for about 10 minutes. Stir in the coriander puree and the lime juice. Taste and season the dish with salt and pepper. Serve with lime wedges and yogurt.

**Per Serving:** Calories 335; Fat: 11.27g; Sodium: 140mg; Carbs: 47.3g; Fibre: 9g; Sugar: 8.35g; Protein: 14.63g

## Lentils & Bulgur

**Prep Time:** 30 minutes | **Cook Time:** 35 minutes | **Serves:** 4-6

60 ml extra-virgin olive oil
2 medium yellow onions, halved and thinly sliced
3 bay leaves
2½ teaspoons ground cumin
½ teaspoon ground allspice
Salt and ground black pepper
180 g coarse bulgur
210 g brown lentils, rinsed and drained
4 spring onions, thinly sliced
10 g chopped fresh flat-leaf parsley
Plain yogurt, to serve

1. Add oil to the pot. Select SEAR/SAUTÉ. Select Lo3, and then press START/STOP to begin cooking. 2. When the oil is shimmering, add the onions and cook them for 20 minutes until deeply browned. 3. Transfer about half the onions to a paper towel–lined plate; set aside. Add the bay, cumin, allspice and 2 teaspoons salt to the pot, and then cook them for 30 seconds until fragrant. Pour in 720 ml water, scraping up any browned bits. 4. Stop the process, and stir in the bulgur and lentils, then distribute in an even layer. 5. Close the lid, turn the pressure release valve to SEAL position, and then move the slider to PRESSURE. Select HI and set the cooking time to 10 minutes. Press START/STOP to begin cooking. When finished, release the pressure quickly. 6. Drape a kitchen towel across the pot and re-cover without locking the lid in place. Let stand for 10 minutes. 7. Open the pot, and then fluff the mixture with a fork, removing and discarding the bay. Taste and season the dish with salt and pepper. Transfer to a serving dish and sprinkle with the reserved onions, the spring onions and parsley. 8. Serve the food with yogurt.

**Per Serving:** Calories 87; Fat: 4.3g; Sodium: 89mg; Carbs: 10.99g; Fibre: 2.3g; Sugar: 0.84g; Protein: 2.89g

## Pecan Bacon Strips

**Prep Time:** 10 minutes | **Cook Time:** 30 minutes | **Serves:** 6

12 bacon strips
55 g packed brown sugar
30 g finely chopped pecans
⅛ tsp. ground cinnamon
⅛ tsp. pepper

1. Line a suitable baking pan with foil. Arrange the bacon strips into the pan in a single layer. 2. Place the pan in the pot. Close the lid and move slider to AIR FRY/STOVETOP, then use the dial to select BAKE/ROAST. Adjust the cooking temperature to 190°C and set the cooking time to 18 minutes. Press START/STOP to begin cooking. 3. Remove the bacon from pan. Discard drippings from pan, wiping clean if necessary. 4. In a shallow bowl, mix remaining ingredients. Dip both sides of bacon in brown sugar mixture, patting to help coating adhere; return to pan. 5. Bake the food for 8 to 10 minutes longer or until caramelized. 6. Serve hot.

**Per Serving:** Calories 95; Fat: 5.93g; Sodium: 149mg; Carbs: 10.27g; Fibre: 0.7g; Sugar: 9.06g; Protein: 1.47g

## Honey "Baked" Cauliflower

**Prep Time:** 10 minutes | **Cook Time:** 10 minutes | **Serves:** 4

240 ml water
1 medium head cauliflower, chopped
120 g plain flour
4 large eggs, lightly beaten
110 g panko bread crumbs
9 tablespoons honey
6 cloves garlic, minced
4 tablespoons soy sauce
1½ tablespoons hot chili sauce

1. Place cauliflower and flour in a zip-topped bag. 2. Shake them until cauliflower is evenly coated with flour. 3. Dip each piece of cauliflower into eggs and then into bread crumbs. Place coated cauliflower in a metal bowl. 4. Combine honey, garlic, soy sauce, and hot chili sauce in the pot, and cook them at Lo1 on SEAR/ SAUTÉ mode for 1 minute, stirring constantly. 5. Pour sauce over cauliflower in the metal bowl. Cover the bowl of cauliflower tightly with foil. 6. Clean inner pot and place back inside the unit. Create a foil sling and carefully lower bowl into pot. 7. Close the lid, turn the pressure release valve to SEAL position, and then move the slider to PRESSURE. Select HI and set the cooking time to 5 minutes. Press START/STOP to begin cooking. When finished, release the pressure quickly. 8. Remove the bowl using foil sling. Take foil off of top of bowl and serve.

**Per Serving:** Calories 406; Fat: 8.23g; Sodium: 318mg; Carbs: 76.68g; Fibre: 3g; Sugar: 44g; Protein: 9.59g

## Cheese Broccoli Risotto

**Prep Time:** 10 minutes | **Cook Time:** 15 minutes | **Serves:** 4

4 tablespoons olive oil
4 tablespoons butter, divided
1 medium head broccoli, chopped
4 cloves garlic, minced
300 g arborio rice
960 ml vegetable stock
100 g shredded Cheddar cheese
½ teaspoon salt
¼ teaspoon black pepper

1. Select SEAR/SAUTÉ. Select Lo3, and then press START/STOP to begin cooking. 2. Add oil and 2 tablespoons butter, and then cook the broccoli in the pot for 4 minutes; add garlic and cook for an additional 30 seconds. 3. Stop the process, then transfer the broccoli and garlic to a bowl and set aside. Stir the rice, stock, and deglaze in the pot. 4. Close the lid, turn the pressure release valve to SEAL position, and then move the slider to PRESSURE. Select HI and set the cooking time to 7 minutes. Press START/STOP to begin cooking. When finished, release the pressure naturally. 5. Mix in broccoli and garlic, remaining 2 tablespoons butter, Cheddar cheese, salt, and pepper. 6. Serve hot.

**Per Serving:** Calories 664; Fat: 49.31g; Sodium: 1868mg; Carbs: 50.13g; Fibre: 12.9g; Sugar: 4.6g; Protein: 20.44g

## Enchilada & Sweet Potato Casserole

**Prep Time:** 10 minutes | **Cook Time:** 15 minutes | **Serves:** 4

2 tablespoons olive oil
½ medium sweet potato, peeled and diced
½ medium yellow onion, peeled and diced
½ medium red pepper, seeded and diced
½ teaspoon salt
¼ teaspoon red pepper flakes
¼ teaspoon dried oregano
¼ teaspoon black pepper
2 cloves garlic, minced
1 can black beans, drained and rinsed
1 (250 g) can red enchilada sauce
4 small corn tortillas
100 g shredded Cheddar cheese
240 ml water

1. Select SEAR/SAUTÉ. Select Lo3, and then press START/STOP to begin cooking. 2. Add sweet potato, onion, pepper, salt, red pepper flakes, oregano, and black pepper to the pot, and cook them for 5 minutes until the sweet potatoes are tender; add garlic and black beans, and cook them for 30 seconds. 3. Stop the process. 4. Pour half can of enchilada sauce on bottom of a cake pan. Place one tortilla over sauce. 5. Scoop ⅓ sweet potato mixture over tortilla and top with another tortilla. Continue for remaining filling and tortillas. Top enchiladas with remaining ½ can sauce and cheese. Cover the cake pan tightly with foil. 6. Clean the pot and insert back. Pour water into the pot and place the rack in it. 7. Create foil sling and carefully lower cake pan into pot. 8. Close the lid, turn the pressure release valve to SEAL position, and then move the slider to PRESSURE. Select HI and set the cooking time to 8 minutes. Press START/STOP to begin cooking. When finished, release the pressure quickly. 9. Remove pan using foil sling and then remove foil from pan and serve.
**Per Serving:** Calories 304; Fat: 19.46g; Sodium: 649mg; Carbs: 23.31g; Fibre: 4.4g; Sugar: 4.96g; Protein: 11.48g

## Cheese Ravioli Casserole

**Prep Time:** 10 minutes | **Cook Time:** 10 minutes | **Serves:** 2

240 ml water
240 g pasta sauce, divided
1 (225 g) package cheese ravioli, cooked
120 g ricotta cheese
25 g Parmesan cheese
1 tablespoon finely chopped Italian parsley

1. Spread 60 g pasta sauce on bottom of a suitable cake pan. 2. Arrange the cooked ravioli in cake pan. Drop spoonfuls of ricotta cheese over ravioli, some ravioli may still peak through. 3. Pour remaining pasta sauce over ravioli and ricotta. Sprinkle Parmesan and parsley over casserole. Cover the cake pan tightly with foil. Create a foil sling. 4. Pour the water in the pot and place the rack in the pot. 5. Carefully lower cake pan into pot. 6. Close the lid, turn the pressure release valve to SEAL position, and then move the slider to PRESSURE. Select HI and set the cooking time to 10 minutes. Press START/STOP to begin cooking. 7. When finished, release the pressure quickly. 8. Remove cake pan using foil sling and then remove foil from cake pan and serve.
**Per Serving:** Calories 297; Fat: 13.61g; Sodium: 1588mg; Carbs: 29.88g; Fibre: 4.1g; Sugar: 10.06g; Protein: 15.76g

## Tomato Tortellini

**Prep Time:** 10 minutes | **Cook Time:** 10 minutes | **Serves:** 4

4 L water
¾ teaspoon salt, divided
1 (475 g) package frozen cheese tortellini
2 tablespoons olive oil
340 g grape tomatoes
4 tablespoons finely chopped basil
2 cloves garlic, minced
½ teaspoon red pepper flakes
¼ teaspoon black pepper
50 g grated Parmesan cheese

1. Pour water into the pot and add ½ teaspoon salt. Bring the water to a boil at Lo3 on SEAR/SAUTÉ mode. 2. Pour in tortellini and boil for 3 minutes until tortellini floats to top of water. Drain water, reserving 240 ml water. Remove tortellini and set aside. 3. Add oil to pot and add tomatoes, and cook them for 5 minutes until tomatoes begin to burst; add the basil, garlic, red pepper, black pepper, and remaining ¼ teaspoon salt, and cook them for 30 seconds; pour in the reserved water, and add tortellini, and Parmesan cheese; stir them for 30 seconds. 4. Serve hot.

**Per Serving:** Calories 621; Fat: 51.05g; Sodium: 1478mg; Carbs: 4.09g; Fibre: 0.2g; Sugar: 1.18g; Protein: 36.84g

## Herb-Loaded Warm Potato Salad

**Prep Time:** 20 minutes | **Cook Time:** 5 minutes | **Serves:** 4

680 g red and yellow baby potatoes, larger potatoes sliced in half
120 ml chicken or vegetable stock
Salt
Freshly ground black pepper
2 tbsp. minced red onion
2 tbsp. white wine vinegar
¼ tsp. sugar
95 g frozen peas
1 tbsp. mayonnaise
1 tbsp. light sour cream
1 tbsp. chopped fresh parsley
1 tsp. chopped fresh dill
¼ tsp. dried oregano
¼ tsp. crushed red pepper flakes

1. Combine the potatoes, stock and a pinch each of salt and pepper in the pot. 2. Close the lid, turn the pressure release valve to SEAL position, and then move the slider to PRESSURE. Select HI and set the cooking time to 2 minutes. Press START/STOP to begin cooking. When finished, release the pressure quickly. 3. Combine the red onion, vinegar and sugar in a small bowl. Let the mixture sit while the potatoes steam. 4. Add the peas, mayonnaise, sour cream, herbs, salt, black pepper, and the red pepper flakes to the pot. Stir in the onion mixture until everything is combined. 5. Let the salad warm for 1 minute. Adjust the salt and pepper to taste. Enjoy.

**Per Serving:** Calories 177; Fat: 3.7g; Sodium: 230mg; Carbs: 32.16g; Fibre: 4.2g; Sugar: 3.07g; Protein: 4.89g

## Stuffed Poblano Peppers

**Prep Time:** 30 minutes | **Cook Time:** 10 minutes | **Serves:** 4-6

6 large poblano peppers
185 g cooked quinoa
85 g drained and rinsed black beans
80 g diced red onion
½ tsp. ground cumin
½ tsp. chili powder
Salt
Freshly ground black pepper
1 tbsp hot sauce
2 tbsp tomato sauce
1 tbsp chopped fresh coriander, plus more for topping
115 g shredded pepper Jack cheese, divided
240 ml water

1. Slice vertically down one side of each poblano, from the stem to the tip, to remove a piece about 5 cm wide, leaving the stem attached. Dice the removed portion, leaving the rest of each pepper intact until ready to stuff. 2. Combine the diced poblano, quinoa, black beans, red onion, cumin, chili powder, salt and black pepper to taste, hot sauce, tomato sauce, coriander and one-quarter of the pepper Jack cheese in a large bowl. 3. Spoon the quinoa mixture into each reserved poblano pepper. Use the back of the spoon to press the filling into each pepper. 4. Once each pepper is filled, pour the water into the pot and insert the rack. Arrange the peppers on the rack. Top the peppers with the remaining cheese. 5. Close the lid, turn the pressure release valve to SEAL position, and then move the slider to PRESSURE. Select HI and set the cooking time to 10 minutes. Press START/STOP to begin cooking. When finished, release the pressure quickly. 6. Remove the lid and use tongs to carefully transfer the peppers individually to plates. Top the cooked peppers with fresh coriander.

**Per Serving:** Calories 158; Fat: 6.74g; Sodium: 250mg; Carbs: 16.95g; Fibre: 3.4g; Sugar: 3.81g; Protein: 8.43g

## Chickpeas with Spinach

**Prep Time:** 5 minutes | **Cook Time:** 35 minutes | **Serves:** 6

165 g dried chickpeas, rinsed
960 ml water
1 (500 g) can tomato sauce
1 teaspoon garlic powder
¼ teaspoon ground ginger
1 tablespoon curry powder
⅛ teaspoon ground nutmeg
½ teaspoon salt
¼ teaspoon ground black pepper
60 g fresh baby spinach

1. Add chickpeas and water to the pot. 2. Close the lid, turn the pressure release valve to SEAL position, and then move the slider to PRESSURE. Select HI and set the cooking time to 30 minutes. Press START/STOP to begin cooking. When finished, release the pressure naturally. 3. Stir in remaining ingredients, and then simmer them at LO on PRESSURE COOK mode for 4 minutes to heat through and wilt spinach. 4. Transfer mixture to a serving dish and serve warm.

**Per Serving:** Calories 151; Fat: 2.48g; Sodium: 329mg; Carbs: 26.04g; Fibre: 6.8g; Sugar: 6.3g; Protein: 8.18g

# Crustless Vegetable Potpie

**Prep Time:** 20 minutes | **Cook Time:** 15 minutes | **Serves:** 4

- 1 large head cauliflower, cut into florets
- 710 ml vegetable or chicken stock
- 130 g frozen peas
- 260 g sliced carrot
- 2 medium Yukon gold potatoes, peeled and diced
- 3 celery ribs, diced
- 1 medium yellow onion, diced
- 3 cloves garlic, minced
- 2 bay leaves
- 1½ tsp sea salt, plus more to taste
- ½ tsp. dried marjoram
- 2 tbsp. fresh thyme, for garnish (optional)

1. Combine the cauliflower florets and stock in the pot. 2. Close the lid, turn the pressure release valve to SEAL position, and then move the slider to PRESSURE. Select HI and set the cooking time to 5 minutes. Press START/STOP to begin cooking. When finished, release the pressure quickly. 3. Using an immersion blender or blender, puree the cauliflower mixture to form the base of your potpie. 4. Add the frozen peas, carrot, potatoes, celery, onion, garlic and bay leaves to the cauliflower mixture. Sprinkle with the salt and marjoram and give the mixture a stir. 5. Cook the food at HI on PRESSURE COOK mode for 7 minutes. Use a quick release and remove the lid. 6. Serve hot and garnish with fresh thyme (optional), and additional salt to taste (if needed).

**Per Serving:** Calories 254; Fat: 2.07g; Sodium: 1860mg; Carbs: 45.3g; Fibre: 7.4g; Sugar: 7.16g; Protein: 15.51g

# Chapter 4 Poultry Mains

## Chicken Sausage Ragu

**Prep Time:** 30 minutes | **Cook Time:** 15 minutes | **Serves:** 4

2 tablespoons olive oil
200 g spicy Italian sausage
1 medium yellow onion, chopped
1 red or green pepper , chopped
1 tablespoon balsamic vinegar
240 g thin marinara sauce
**Optional garnish**
50 g shaved Parmesan cheese curls

60 ml store-bought chicken stock , or homemade
300 g boneless, skinless chicken thighs, fat trimmed, cut into 5 cm pieces
Salt and freshly ground black pepper
90 g polenta (not quick-cooking)

1. Add 1 tablespoon of the oil to the pot. Select SEAR/SAUTÉ. Select Lo3, and then press START/STOP to begin cooking. 2. When the oil is hot, add the sausages and cook them for 3 minutes until browned; add the onion and pepper , and cook then for 4 minutes until tender. Stop the process. 3. Add the vinegar and scrape up the browned bits on the bottom of a suitable baking pan. Add the marinara sauce and stock and stir to combine. Season the chicken all over with salt and pepper. Add it to the pot and stir to combine. 4. Place the rack in the pot over the chicken. Place 680 ml warm water, the remaining 1 tablespoon oil, and ½ teaspoon salt in the pan. Gradually whisk in the polenta. Cover the pan tightly with foil and place on the rack. 5. Close the lid, turn the pressure release valve to SEAL position, and then move the slider to PRESSURE. Select HI and set the cooking time to 8 minutes. Press START/STOP to begin cooking. When finished, release the pressure naturally. 6. Remove the lid, and blot the top of the foil on the baking dish with a paper towel to remove any water. Carefully lift the baking dish out of the pot, remove the foil, and stir the polenta. 7. Remove the rack from the pot. 8. Serve the polenta in shallow bowls, topped with the chicken ragu and garnished with the cheese curls, if desired.
**Per Serving:** Calories 436; Fat: 23.04g; Sodium: 881mg; Carbs: 39.18g; Fibre: 6.2g; Sugar: 11.49g; Protein: 20.92g

## Chicken Sausage Gumbo

**Prep Time:** 30 minutes | **Cook Time:** 25 minutes | **Serves:** 8

| | |
|---|---|
| 60 ml vegetable oil | 3 bay leaves |
| 30 g plain flour | 2 tablespoons fileé powder |
| 4 stalks celery, chopped | 2 teaspoons Worcestershire sauce |
| 1 large yellow onion, peeled and diced | 1 teaspoon hot sauce |
| 1 large green pepper, seeded and diced | 960 ml chicken stock |
| 110 g sliced fresh okra | 455 g smoked sausage, sliced |
| 4 cloves garlic, peeled and minced | 280 g shredded cooked chicken |
| 1 can diced tomatoes | ¼ teaspoon salt |
| ½ teaspoon dried thyme | ¼ teaspoon ground black pepper |
| ½ teaspoon Creole seasoning | 500 g cooked long-grain rice |

1. Add the oil to the pot. Select SEAR/SAUTÉ. Select Lo3, and then press START/STOP to begin cooking. 2. When the oil is hot, add flour and cook for 15 minutes until flour is medium brown in color; add celery, onion, green pepper, okra, garlic, and tomatoes, and cook them for 8 minutes until tender; add thyme, Creole seasoning, bay leaves, fileé, Worcestershire sauce, hot sauce, and stock and stir them well, making sure nothing is stuck to the bottom of the pot. 3. Add sausage to the pot and stop the process. 4. Close the lid, turn the pressure release valve to SEAL position, and then move the slider to PRESSURE. Select HI and set the cooking time to 8 minutes. Press START/STOP to begin cooking. When finished, release the pressure quickly. 5. Open lid, discard bay leaves, and stir in chicken, salt, and black pepper. Let stand on Keep Warm setting for 10 minutes. 6. Serve the dish hot over rice.

**Per Serving:** Calories 624; Fat: 37.51g; Sodium: 1195mg; Carbs: 28.47g; Fibre: 4.9g; Sugar: 3.34g; Protein: 45.17g

## Chicken Lettuce Wraps

**Prep Time:** 20 minutes | **Cook Time:** 15 minutes | **Serves:** 4

| | |
|---|---|
| 120 ml chicken stock | 30 g crumbled blue cheese |
| 905 g boneless, skinless chicken breast | 2 green onions, chopped |
| 120 g buffalo wing sauce | 8 large lettuce leaves |
| 50 g chopped celery | Ranch or blue cheese dressing, for drizzling |

1. Pour the chicken stock into the pot, and then add the chicken breast. 2. Close the lid, turn the pressure release valve to SEAL position, and then move the slider to PRESSURE. Select HI and set the cooking time to 6 minutes. Press START/STOP to begin cooking. When finished, release the pressure naturally. 3. Mix together the wing sauce, celery, blue cheese and green onions in a medium bowl. 4. Remove the chicken from the pot, chop the chicken and mix it with the sauce mixture. 5. Divide the buffalo chicken among the lettuce leaves, then drizzle with dressing.

**Per Serving:** Calories 720; Fat: 18.22g; Sodium: 1279mg; Carbs: 110.47g; Fibre: 22.7g; Sugar: 55.86g; Protein: 37.9g

## Pesto Chicken Pieces with Quinoa

**Prep Time:** 20 minutes | **Cook Time:** 5 minutes | **Serves:** 5

175 g uncooked quinoa, rinsed
355 ml chicken stock
½ tsp. salt, plus more to taste
455 g chicken breast, cut into bite-size pieces
175 g homemade or store-bought pesto, divided (see note)
150 g sliced cherry tomatoes
35 g fresh Parmesan cheese, for garnish
Mixed greens, for serving

1. Combine the quinoa, chicken stock, salt, chicken breast and half of the pesto in the pot. 2. Close the lid, turn the pressure release valve to SEAL position, and then move the slider to PRESSURE. Select HI and set the cooking time to 1 minute. Press START/STOP to begin cooking. When finished, release the pressure naturally. 3. Open the lid and fluff the quinoa with a fork. 4. Serve with sliced tomatoes, remaining pesto, Parmesan cheese and additional salt, if needed. 5. Alternatively, this recipe can be made ahead and stored in the fridge. 6. Serve warm or at room temperature over a bed of greens.

**Per Serving:** Calories 355; Fat: 13.22g; Sodium: 519mg; Carbs: 30.14g; Fibre: 3.1g; Sugar: 4.85g; Protein: 27.9g

## Veggie Chicken Casserole

**Prep Time:** 10 minutes | **Cook Time:** 15 minutes | **Serves:** 4

1 (700 g) can red enchilada sauce
455 g boneless skinless chicken breast, diced into 1 cm pieces
480 ml chicken stock
1 (375 g) can pink beans, drained and rinsed
1 large green pepper, stemmed, cored, and cut into thin strips
120 g fresh or frozen corn kernels (if frozen, do not thaw)
1 small yellow onion, chopped
1 teaspoon mild smoked paprika
1 teaspoon ground cumin
200 g dried ziti
2 tablespoons yellow polenta

1. Mix the enchilada sauce, chicken, stock, beans, pepper, corn, onion, smoked paprika, and cumin in the pot. Stir in the ziti until coated. 2. Close the lid, turn the pressure release valve to SEAL position, and then move the slider to PRESSURE. Select HI and set the cooking time to 7 minutes. Press START/STOP to begin cooking. When finished, release the pressure quickly. 3. Remove the lid, and select SEAR/SAUTÉ. Select Lo3, and then press START/STOP to begin cooking. 4. Bring the sauce to a simmer, stirring constantly. Add the cornmeal and continue cooking for about 1 minute until thickened, stirring constantly. 5. Stop the process, then cover the lid and let the dish stand for 5 minutes to blend the flavors and continue to thicken the sauce. 6. Stir the dish well before serving.

**Per Serving:** Calories 626; Fat: 16.49g; Sodium: 1287mg; Carbs: 65.34g; Fibre: 10.3g; Sugar: 40.12g; Protein: 56.66g

## Duck Chunks with Potato Cubes

**Prep Time:** 25 minutes | **Cook Time:** 30 minutes | **Serves:** 4-6

1 whole duck (medium), chopped into chunks
2 tbsp. olive oil
4 cloves garlic, minced
4 potatoes, chopped into cubes
2 green onions cut into 5 cm in length
5 cm ginger root, sliced
4 tbsp. sugar
4 tbsp. soy sauce
4 tbsp. rice wine
½ tsp. salt
240 ml water

1. Add the oil to the pot. Select SEAR/SAUTÉ. Select Lo3, and then press START/STOP to begin cooking. 2. When the oil is hot, add the duck and cook until the duck has turned light brown. 3. Stop the process and add all of the ingredients except the potatoes to the pot. 4. Close the lid, turn the pressure release valve to SEAL position, and then move the slider to PRESSURE. Select HI and set the cooking time to 25 minutes. Press START/STOP to begin cooking. 5. Add the potatoes cubes to the pot after 20 minutes of cooking time. 6. When finished, release the pressure naturally. 7. Serve warm.

**Per Serving:** Calories 510; Fat: 20.43g; Sodium: 430mg; Carbs: 60.17g; Fibre: 6.7g; Sugar: 14.86g; Protein: 22.48g

## Garlic–Lemon Turkey Breast

**Prep Time:** 20 minutes | **Cook Time:** 40 minutes | **Serves:** 4-6

1 tbsp. extra-virgin olive oil
30 g unsalted butter, at room temperature
1 (1.4-kg) turkey breast, spine and neck removed
2 tbsp chopped fresh rosemary
Zest of 1 lemon
2 cloves garlic, grated
Salt
Freshly ground black pepper
240 ml water

1. Pour the olive oil onto the turkey. Rub the butter all over and even under the skin of the turkey breast. 2. Sprinkle the rosemary, lemon zest, garlic and generous amounts of salt and pepper all over the turkey breast. 3. Rub the seasonings all over the turkey and under the skin. 4. Pour the water into the pot and insert the rack. Place the turkey on top of the rack, breast/skin side up and bone side down. 5. Close the lid, turn the pressure release valve to SEAL position, and then move the slider to PRESSURE. Select HI and set the cooking time to 25 minutes. Press START/STOP to begin cooking. When finished, release the pressure naturally. 6. Line a large baking sheet with foil. Carefully transfer the turkey breast to the prepared baking sheet. 7. Bake the turkey breast in the oven for 15 minutes until the skin is nice and golden and crispy. 8. Let the turkey rest for 10 minutes before removing the meat from the bones and then slicing.

**Per Serving:** Calories 151; Fat: 8.75g; Sodium: 2424mg; Carbs: 1g; Fibre: 0.1g; Sugar: 0.21g; Protein: 16.25g

## Tangy Thai Basil Orange Chicken

**Prep Time:** 20 minutes | **Cook Time:** 20 minutes | **Serves:** 4-6

- 2 tbsp. grass-fed butter, ghee or avocado oil
- 1 large shallot, thinly sliced
- 5 cloves garlic, finely chopped
- 2.5-cm chunk fresh ginger, peeled and finely minced or grated
- ¾ tsp. sea salt
- ¼ tsp. red pepper flakes (optional)
- 60 ml honey
- 175 ml freshly squeezed orange juice
- 60 ml cider vinegar
- 2 tbsp coconut aminos
- 2 tsp. Asian fish sauce
- 905 g boneless, skinless chicken breast
- 25 g fresh Thai basil leaves, plus more for garnish
- 25 g finely chopped fresh mint

1. Add the healthy fat of choice to the pot. 2. Select SEAR/SAUTÉ. Select Lo3, and then press START/STOP to begin cooking. 3. When the fat is melted, add the shallot and sauté for 3 minutes or until fragrant; add the garlic and ginger and sauté them for 2 minutes. 4. Stop the process, and add the salt, red pepper flakes (optional), honey, orange juice, vinegar, coconut aminos, fish sauce and chicken to the pot, and give the mixture a stir, making sure the chicken is submerged in the liquid. 5. Close the lid, turn the pressure release valve to SEAL position, and then move the slider to PRESSURE. Select HI and set the cooking time to 9 minutes. Press START/STOP to begin cooking. When finished, release the pressure naturally. 6. Transfer the chicken to a plate or cutting board. Cut the chicken into bite-size chunks, and then set aside. 7. Simmer the liquid in the pot at Lo2 on SEAR/SAUTÉ mode for 5 minutes or until the liquid slightly thickens. 8. Stop the process, and add the shredded chicken, Thai basil and mint to the pot, then stir them a few times until the fresh herbs have wilted into the sauce, then allow the mixture to rest for 10 minutes. 9. Garnish the dish with fresh Thai basil leaves and enjoy.

**Per Serving:** Calories 368; Fat: 11.97g; Sodium: 864mg; Carbs: 48.52g; Fibre: 2.6g; Sugar: 22.8g; Protein: 16.49g

## Turkey Salsa Verde

**Prep Time:** 20 minutes | **Cook Time:** 20 minutes | **Serves:** 4-6

- 1.2 kg turkey breast, chopped into cubes (3.5 cm)
- 400 g salsa verde
- ¼ tsp. smoked paprika
- ¼ tsp. garlic salt
- ¼ tsp. ground black pepper
- ¼ tsp. turmeric
- ¼ tsp. cumin

1. Combine the salsa, turmeric, cumin, paprika, salt, and pepper in the pot. 2. Put the turkey cubes in the pot and toss until turkey is covered in sauce. 3. Close the lid, turn the pressure release valve to SEAL position, and then move the slider to PRESSURE. Select HI and set the cooking time to 20 minutes. Press START/STOP to begin cooking. When finished, release the pressure quickly. 4. Serve.

**Per Serving:** Calories 321; Fat: 13.44g; Sodium: 645mg; Carbs: 5.48g; Fibre: 1.5g; Sugar: 3.09g; Protein: 42.62g

## Mushroom & Chicken Chunk Stroganoff

**Prep Time:** 20 minutes | **Cook Time:** 25 minutes | **Serves:** 4

2 tbsp. avocado oil or olive oil
675 g chicken breast, cut into 2.5- to 5-cm chunks
2 tbsp cornflour plus more if needed
340 g Portobello mushrooms, sliced
3 cloves garlic, minced
2 tbsp coconut aminos or soy sauce
1 tbsp cider vinegar
175 ml chicken stock
120 ml full-fat canned coconut milk or coconut cream
Salt
Cooked rice, cauliflower rice or pasta, for serving
3 tbsp. (8 g) chopped fresh basil or (12 g) parsley, for garnish (optional)

1. In a resealable plastic bag, toss the chicken and cornflour together. Shake it up so that the chicken is completely covered. 2. Add the oil to the pot. Select SEAR/SAUTÉ. Select Lo3, and then press START/STOP to begin cooking. 3. When the oil is hot, add the chicken chunks and cook them for 1 to 2 minutes on each side or until they are slightly browned. 4. Stop the process, and then toss in the mushrooms and garlic. 5. In a small bowl, stir together the coconut aminos, vinegar and chicken stock. Pour on top of the chicken mixture. 6. Close the lid, turn the pressure release valve to SEAL position, and then move the slider to PRESSURE. Select HI and set the cooking time to 7 minutes. Press START/STOP to begin cooking. When finished, release the pressure naturally. 7. If the sauce seems too thin, add another tablespoon of tapioca starch to the coconut milk. Pour the coconut milk into the pot and mix until well incorporated. 8. Cook the food at Lo3 on SEAR/SAUTÉ again for another 10 minutes or until the mixture is creamy. 9. Season the mixture with salt and stop the process. 10. Spoon the mixture on top of rice, cauliflower rice or pasta and serve immediately, garnished with the fresh basil or parsley.
**Per Serving:** Calories 746; Fat: 34.43g; Sodium: 482mg; Carbs: 73.07g; Fibre: 10.7g; Sugar: 3.06g; Protein: 46.66g

## Turkey Breast Casserole

**Prep Time:** 15 minutes | **Cook Time:** 35 minutes | **Serves:** 6

900 g boneless turkey breast, about 4 pieces
1 medium-sized onion, sliced
1 celery stalk, sliced
1 bag (250 g) frozen mixed vegetables
½ tsp. salt
½ tsp. ground black pepper
240 g chicken stock
2 small cans of creamy mushroom soup
1 bag (350 g) herb stuffing mix

1. Season the turkey breast with salt and pepper. 2. Add the onion, celery, frozen mixed vegetables, and turkey breast to the pot, and then pour in the stock. 3. Close the lid, turn the pressure release valve to SEAL position, and then move the slider to PRESSURE. Select HI and set the cooking time to 25 minutes. Press START/STOP to begin cooking. When finished, release the pressure quickly. 4. Pour the mushroom soup into the pot and add stuffing mix, then cook them at Lo3 on SEAR/SAUTÉ mode for 8 minutes more, stirring occasionally. 5. Transfer cooked turkey to a serving bowl and drizzle with the sauce. Serve.
**Per Serving:** Calories 387; Fat: 15.88g; Sodium: 1227mg; Carbs: 10.99g; Fibre: 2g; Sugar: 1.48g; Protein: 47.62g

# Tikka Chicken Masala

**Prep Time:** 20 minutes | **Cook Time:** 20 minutes | **Serves:** 5-6

2 tbsp. avocado oil or extra-virgin olive oil
1 (2.5-cm) piece ginger, peeled and chopped
1 small onion, chopped
3 cloves garlic, minced
2 tsp paprika
1 tsp. garam masala
1 tsp. ground turmeric
2 tsp ground cumin
1 tsp. ground coriander
¼ tsp. cayenne pepper (optional)
120 ml chicken stock
1 (410 g) can diced tomatoes, with juice
680 g boneless skinless chicken breast
120 ml canned coconut milk
1 tbsp cornflour (optional)
2 tbsp fresh lemon juice
Salt
Chopped fresh basil or coriander (optional)
745 g cooked rice, for serving

1. Select SEAR/SAUTÉ. Select Lo3, and then press START/STOP to begin cooking. 2. Add the oil, ginger, onion and garlic to the pot, and cook them for 3 to 4 minutes or until the onion is translucent. 3. Stop the process, and add paprika, garam masala, turmeric, cumin, coriander and cayenne (optional) to the top, scraping the bottom of the pot to form a paste. 4. Pour in the chicken stock to deglaze the pot; this also helps prevent burning when the dish comes to pressure. Add the tomatoes, and then nestle the chicken on top. 5. Close the lid, turn the pressure release valve to SEAL position, and then move the slider to PRESSURE. Select HI and set the cooking time to 7 minutes. Press START/STOP to begin cooking. When finished, release the pressure naturally. 6. Remove the lid and chop the chicken. Return the chicken to the pot. Simmer them at Lo1 on SEAR/SAUTÉ for 4 to 5 minutes. Add the coconut milk. If the mixture is too thin, add the cornflour to the lemon juice before adding the juice to the mixture. 7. Season the dish with salt to taste, and once the mixture is thick, serve immediately with fresh basil or coriander (optional) over rice.

**Per Serving:** Calories 509; Fat: 29.42g; Sodium: 199mg; Carbs: 47.71g; Fibre: 19.1g; Sugar: 4.31g; Protein: 38.11g

# Orange Chicken Thighs & Vegetables

**Prep Time:** 10 minutes | **Cook Time:** 25 minutes | **Serves:** 4

Juice and zest from 1 orange (80 ml juice and about ½ tablespoon zest)
115 g pure maple syrup (see this page)
80 ml soy sauce or tamari
3 tablespoons raw apple cider vinegar
1 tablespoon minced fresh ginger (about 2.5 cm knob), or ½ teaspoon dried ginger
1 clove garlic, minced, or ¼ teaspoon ground garlic
¼ teaspoon red pepper flakes
455 g boneless, skinless chicken thighs
200 g white jasmine rice, rinsed
240 ml plus 2 tablespoons water
½ red onion, thinly sliced
1 red pepper, seeded and sliced
200 g chopped broccoli florets
1 tablespoon cornflour
Chopped green onion and sesame seeds, for garnish (optional)

1. Combine the orange juice and zest, maple syrup, soy sauce, vinegar, ginger, garlic, and red pepper flakes in the pot. 2. Place the chicken thighs on top of the sauce. Arrange the rack over the chicken and place an oven-safe bowl on top. Add the rice and 240 ml of the water to the bowl. 3. Close the lid, turn the pressure release valve to SEAL position, and then move the slider to PRESSURE. Select HI and set the cooking time to 12 minutes. Press START/STOP to begin cooking. When finished, release the pressure quickly. 4. Lift the rack and the bowl out of the pot. Fluff the rice with a fork. Transfer the chicken to a cutting board. 5. Select SEAR/SAUTÉ. Select Lo2, and then press START/STOP to begin cooking. 6. Add onion, pepper, and broccoli to the pot, and cook them for 8 minutes until the vegetables are fork-tender. 7. In a small bowl, stir together the cornflour and the remaining 2 tablespoons water to make slurry. 8. Cut the chicken into bite-sized chunks and stir them into the simmering sauce. Add the slurry to the pot and stir well. The sauce will thicken and become glossy within 1 to 2 minutes. 9. Serve the orange chicken warm over the rice with green onion and sesame seeds sprinkled on top. 10. You can store the leftovers in an airtight container in the fridge for 3 or 4 days.

**Per Serving:** Calories 472; Fat: 6.91g; Sodium: 1646mg; Carbs: 84.34g; Fibre: 4g; Sugar: 23.13g; Protein: 17.14g

## Carrot Chicken Tikka Masala

**Prep Time:** 15 minutes | **Cook Time:** 15 minutes | **Serves:** 6

1 yellow onion, chopped
1 can diced tomatoes
1 teaspoon garam masala
1 teaspoon ground cumin
1 tablespoon ground coriander
1 teaspoon paprika
¼ teaspoon ground cinnamon
¼ teaspoon ground ginger
¼ teaspoon cayenne pepper (optional)
1 tablespoon pure maple syrup
675 g boneless, skinless chicken thighs
2 teaspoons fine sea salt
200 g long-grain white rice, like jasmine or basmati
300 ml water
½ head cauliflower, chopped
3 peeled, chopped carrots
120 ml full-fat canned coconut milk

1. Combine the onion, tomatoes with their juices, garam masala, cumin, coriander, paprika, cinnamon, ginger, cayenne, and maple syrup in the pot and use an immersion blender to blend until smooth. 2. Place the chicken on top of the sauce and season it with the salt. Arrange the rack over the chicken and place an oven-safe bowl on top. Add the rice and water to the bowl. 3. Close the lid, turn the pressure release valve to SEAL position, and then move the slider to PRESSURE. Select HI and set the cooking time to 12 minutes. Press START/STOP to begin cooking. When finished, release the pressure naturally. 4. Lift the rack and the bowl of cooked rice out of the pot. Fluff the rice with a fork. Transfer the cooked chicken to a cutting board. Add the cauliflower and carrots to the sauce. Cook them at HI on PRESSURE COOK mode for 1 minute, and release the steam pressure quickly. 5. Cut the chicken into bite-sized pieces and stir them into the sauce. Stir in the coconut milk, then taste and adjust the seasonings as needed. Serve warm over the rice. 6. You can store the leftovers in an airtight container in the fridge for 3 or 4 days.
**Per Serving:** Calories 426; Fat: 13.62g; Sodium: 1273mg; Carbs: 61.98g; Fibre: 6.9g; Sugar: 14.79g; Protein: 15.24g

## Turkey Breast Roast in Chicken Stock

**Prep Time:** 20 minutes | **Cook Time:** 40 minutes | **Serves:** 4

1 (1.3 kg.) turkey breast roast, boneless
2 tbsp. + 2 tsp. garlic infused oil
2 tsp. salt
360 ml chicken stock

1. Rub all sides of the turkey with 2 tablespoons of oil and season with salt. 2. Add the remaining oil to the pot. Select SEAR/SAUTÉ. Select Lo3, and then press START/STOP to begin cooking. 3. When the oil is hot, put the meat in the pot and brown on both sides. 4. Stop the process, and transfer the turkey breast roast to a bowl. 5. Add the stock to the pot and deglaze the pot by scraping the bottom to remove all of the brown bits; place the rack in the pot and place the meat on it. 6. Close the lid, turn the pressure release valve to SEAL position, and then move the slider to PRESSURE. Select HI and set the cooking time to 30 minutes. Press START/STOP to begin cooking. When finished, release the pressure naturally. 7. Serve.
**Per Serving:** Calories 681; Fat: 15.82g; Sodium: 1883mg; Carbs: 0.69g; Fibre: 0g; Sugar: 0g; Protein: 125.88g

# Onion Chicken Shawarma

**Prep Time:** 10 minutes | **Cook Time:** 10 minutes | **Serves:** 4-6

120 ml extra-virgin olive oil
2 tablespoons salted butter
1 yellow onion, sliced lengthwise into 2.5 cm wedges
3 cloves garlic, minced or pressed
1.8 kg boneless, skinless chicken thighs, cut into 0.5 cm strips
1 tablespoon paprika
1 tablespoon curry powder
1 tablespoon seasoned salt
2 teaspoons black pepper
1½ teaspoons ground cumin
1 teaspoon turmeric
1 teaspoon cinnamon
½–1 teaspoon cayenne pepper (optional)
½–1 teaspoon crushed red pepper flakes (optional)
120 ml garlic stock or chicken stock

**TO SERVE**
Pita/flatbread warmed or room temperature
Hummus
Red onion, thinly sliced
Dill or sour pickles, diced
Tzatziki

1. Add olive oil and butter to the pot. Select SEAR/SAUTÉ. Select Lo3, and then press START/STOP to begin cooking. 2. When the butter melted, add the onion and garlic, and sauté them for about 3 minutes until slightly softened; add the chicken thighs, paprika, curry powder, seasoned salt, black pepper, cumin, turmeric, cinnamon, cayenne pepper (optional), and crushed red pepper flakes (optional), and stir to coat everything in the spices. 3. Stop the process and stir in the stock, scraping up any browned bits from the bottom of the pot. 4. Close the lid, turn the pressure release valve to SEAL position, and then move the slider to PRESSURE. Select HI and set the cooking time to 7 minutes. Press START/STOP to begin cooking. When finished, release the pressure quickly. 5. Prepare the shawarma wrap by yourself. Take some pita, spread on some hummus, and layer with chicken and onions from the pot as well as sliced red onion, pickles, and tzatziki. Finish by drizzling the incredible spice-infused oil from the pot over the top. 6. Roll it up tightly (wrapping the sandwich in foil may help with any messy drippings) and enjoy!

**Per Serving:** Calories 678; Fat: 29.4g; Sodium: 2232mg; Carbs: 69.33g; Fibre: 6.7g; Sugar: 17.68g; Protein: 33.49g

## Turkey Breast with Vegetables

**Prep Time:** 10 minutes | **Cook Time:** 35 minutes | **Serves:** 4-6

3 tablespoons extra-virgin olive oil
1 tablespoon dried sage
1 teaspoon dried thyme
1½ teaspoons paprika
1 teaspoon dried tarragon
1 teaspoon seasoned salt
2 teaspoons pepper
3 cloves garlic, minced or pressed
1 (1.8 – 2.2 kg) turkey breast (bone-in or boneless), thawed, rinsed, and timer removed (if it came with one)
480 ml turkey or chicken stock
1–2 small yellow onions, quartered
2 large carrots, peeled and sliced into 1 cm disks
3 ribs celery, sliced
2 tablespoons cornflour
A few drops Gravy Master or Kitchen Bouquet (optional)
2 packets gravy mix (optional)

1. Mix together the olive oil, sage, thyme, paprika, tarragon, seasoned salt, pepper, and garlic in a bowl. Set aside. 2. Place the turkey breast on the rack with breast side up, and carefully lower into the pot. Use a silicone brush to apply the spice mixture all over the turkey. 3. Pour in the stock, and then add the onions, carrots, and celery, arranging them around the side of the turkey breast. 4. Close the lid, turn the pressure release valve to SEAL position, and then move the slider to PRESSURE. Select HI and set the cooking time to 35 minutes. Press START/STOP to begin cooking. When finished, release the pressure naturally. 5. Transfer the turkey breast to a serving dish and leave everything else in the pot. 6. Mix the cornflour with 2 tablespoons water to form slurry. Set aside. 7. Stir the Gravy Master (optional) and gravy packets (optional) in the pot, and cook them at Hi5 on SEAR/SAUTÉ mode. Once the contents begin to bubble, immediately stir in the cornflour slurry and simmer for 30 seconds. 8. Let the gravy stand until thickened. 9. Carve the turkey into slices against the grain of the meat and serve, topped with the gravy.
**Per Serving:** Calories 687; Fat: 14.14g; Sodium: 1065mg; Carbs: 7.05g; Fibre: 1g; Sugar: 1.5g; Protein: 125.32g

## Veggie & Duck Chunks

**Prep Time:** 35 minutes | **Cook Time:** 20 minutes | **Serves:** 4-6

1 whole duck (medium), chopped into chunks
1½ tsp. salt
½ tsp. black pepper
2 carrots cut into pieces
1 cucumber cut into pieces
2.5 cm ginger pieces, chopped
240 ml water
1½ tbsp. red wine

1. Rub all sides of the duck pieces with salt and pepper, and then transfer them to the pot. 2. Add the carrot, cucumber, ginger, water, and wine to the pot. 3. Close the lid, turn the pressure release valve to SEAL position, and then move the slider to PRESSURE. Select HI and set the cooking time to 20 minutes. Press START/STOP to begin cooking. When finished, release the pressure naturally. 4. Serve.
**Per Serving:** Calories 201; Fat: 13.77g; Sodium: 642mg; Carbs: 2.15g; Fibre: 0.8g; Sugar: 0.99g; Protein: 16.02g

# Chicken Scarpariello

**Prep Time:** 10 minutes | **Cook Time:** 25 minutes | **Serves:** 4-6

60 ml extra-virgin olive oil
1.3 kg boneless or bone-in, skinless chicken thighs
4 tablespoons salted butter
1 large Vidalia (sweet) onion, diced
455 g baby bella mushrooms, sliced
6 cloves garlic, minced
455 g sweet or hot Italian sausage, with casings, sliced into 1 cm-thick pieces
180 ml Marsala wine (dry)
60 ml chicken stock
1 teaspoon dried rosemary
1 teaspoon dried thyme
1 teaspoon Italian seasoning
1 teaspoon seasoned salt
2½ tablespoons cornflour
60 g heavy cream
1 (300 g) jar roasted red peppers, drained and sliced into ½ cm strips
50 g grated Parmesan cheese

1. Select SEAR/SAUTÉ. Select Hi5, and then press START/STOP to begin cooking. 2. Add the olive oil to the pot and heat for 3 minutes; add the chicken thighs and sauté for 30 seconds on each side until lightly seared but not cooked, constantly moving the thighs around so they don't stick to the pot too much. You may cook them in batches. 3. Transfer the chicken thighs to a plate to rest. 4. Add the butter and onion, and as the butter melts, scrape the bottom of the pot of most chicken bits; add the mushrooms and garlic and sauté for 3 minutes, until just softened; add the sausage and sauté for 2 minutes; pour in the Marsala wine and bring to a simmer, once more scraping the bottom of the pot to free it of most browned bits. 5. Stir in the stock, rosemary, thyme, Italian seasoning, and seasoned salt. Place the chicken back in the pot, resting on top of everything. Stop the process. 6. Close the lid, turn the pressure release valve to SEAL position, and then move the slider to PRESSURE. Select HI and set the cooking time to 6 minutes. Press START/STOP to begin cooking. When finished, release the pressure quickly. 7. Remove the chicken thighs to a serving dish to rest. 8. Make cornflour slurry by mixing the cornflour with 2½ tablespoons cold water. Set aside. 9. Stir in the cream and roasted red peppers. Hit Keep Warm/Cancel and then Sauté and Adjust so it's on the High or More setting. 10. Once it begins to bubble, immediately stir in the cornflour slurry and Parmesan. 11. Let simmer for 30 seconds, turn off the pot, and let stand for 5 minutes to let the sauce thicken before draping over the chicken.

**Per Serving:** Calories 911; Fat: 32.26g; Sodium: 1907mg; Carbs: 118.01g; Fibre: 13.3g; Sugar: 17.89g; Protein: 46.43g

## Ketchup Chicken Wings

**Prep Time:** 10 minutes | **Cook Time:** 15-25 minutes | **Serves:** 4-6

240 g ketchup
240 ml apple cider vinegar
210 g packed light-brown sugar
80 g yellow mustard
1 tablespoon onion powder
1 teaspoon garlic powder
½ teaspoon chili powder
¼ teaspoon salt
1 tablespoon honey
1.2 kg chicken wings/wingettes/drumettes
2 tablespoons cornflour

1. Whisk together the ketchup, vinegar, brown sugar, mustard, onion powder, garlic powder, chili powder, salt, and honey in the pot. 2. Select SEAR/SAUTÉ. Select Hi5, and then press START/STOP to begin cooking. 3. Bring the mixture just to a simmer and stop the process, and then place the rack in the pot and rest the chicken wings on it. 4. Close the lid, turn the pressure release valve to SEAL position, and then move the slider to PRESSURE. Select HI and set the cooking time to 8 minutes. Press START/STOP to begin cooking. When finished, release the pressure quickly. 5. Mix the cornflour with 2 tablespoons water to form slurry. Set aside. 6. Transfer the wings to a foil-lined baking sheet, remove the rack, and then bring that amazing tangy BBQ sauce to a bubble at Hi5 on SEAR/SAUTÉ mode. Once it does, immediately stir in the cornflour slurry, mix well, and let bubble for 30 seconds. 7. Let the sauce cool for 5 minutes until it stops bubbling and thickens nicely. 8. Brush the sauce on the wings and, for optimal results, you can grill them in the oven for 5 to 10 minutes until slightly crisped and caramelized.
**Per Serving:** Calories 784; Fat: 38.38g; Sodium: 1514mg; Carbs: 54.81g; Fibre: 1g; Sugar: 47.35g; Protein: 52.46g

## Glazed Whole Turkey

**Prep Time:** 20 minutes | **Cook Time:** 40 minutes | **Serves:** 8-10

4 kg turkey
150 g apricot jam
½ tsp. cumin
½ tsp. turmeric
½ tsp. coriander
1 tsp. salt
1 tsp. ground black pepper
480 ml chicken stock
1 onion, peeled and diced
1 diced carrot

1. Rinse the turkey and dry with paper towels. 2. Combine the jam, cumin, turmeric, coriander, salt and pepper in a bowl. 3. Rub all sides of the turkey with the paste. 4. Pour the stock into the pot, and add the onion, carrot, and the turkey. 5. Close the lid, turn the pressure release valve to SEAL position, and then move the slider to PRESSURE. Select HI and set the cooking time to 40 minutes. Press START/STOP to begin cooking. When finished, release the pressure naturally. 6. Serve. If desired, broil the dish in the oven for a few minutes for a browned top.
**Per Serving:** Calories 882; Fat: 66.02g; Sodium: 690mg; Carbs: 12.34g; Fibre: 1.5g; Sugar: 6.15g; Protein: 55.92g

# Savory Turkey Wings

**Prep Time:** 25 minutes | **Cook Time:** 30 minutes | **Serves:** 4

4 turkey wings
2 tbsp. vegetable oil
2 tbsp. butter
1 tsp. salt
½ tsp. ground black pepper

1 yellow onions, sliced
325 g cranberries
120 g walnuts
1 bunch thyme, roughly chopped
240 ml orange juice

1. Season the turkey wings with salt and pepper. 2. Add the oil to the pot. Select SEAR/SAUTÉ. Select Lo3, and then press START/STOP to begin cooking. 3. When the oil is hot, add the butter and melt it; add the turkey wings and brown them on both sides, and then transfer them to a plate. 4. Add onion, cranberries, walnuts, and thyme to the pot, and sauté them for 2 minutes. 5. Stop the process and pour in the orange juice, then return the turkey wings to the pot and stir them well. 6. Close the lid, turn the pressure release valve to SEAL position, and then move the slider to PRESSURE. Select HI and set the cooking time to 20 minutes. Press START/STOP to begin cooking. When finished, release the pressure naturally. 7. Transfer the turkey to a serving bowl. 8. Simmer the cranberry mix at Lo2 on SEAR/SAUTÉ mode for 5 minutes until the sauce begins to thicken. 9. Serve turkey wings with cranberry sauce.

**Per Serving:** Calories 837; Fat: 57.34g; Sodium: 772mg; Carbs: 24.92g; Fibre: 1.9g; Sugar: 17.99g; Protein: 55.6g

# Chapter 5 Seafood Mains

## Onion Prawns Gumbo

**Prep Time:** 25 minutes | **Cook Time:** 16 minutes | **Serves:** 8

60 ml vegetable oil
30 g plain flour
4 stalks celery, chopped
1 large yellow onion, peeled and diced
1 large green pepper, seeded and diced
2 cloves garlic, peeled and minced
1 (400 g) can diced tomatoes
¼ teaspoon dried thyme
¼ teaspoon cayenne pepper
2 bay leaves
1 tablespoon fileé powder
2 teaspoons Worcestershire sauce
960 ml seafood stock
455 g smoked sausage, sliced
455 g medium prawns, peeled and deveined
¼ teaspoon salt
¼ teaspoon ground black pepper
400 g cooked long-grain rice

1. Add the oil to the pot. Select SEAR/SAUTÉ. Select Lo3, and then press START/STOP to begin cooking. 2. When the oil is hot, add flour and cook for 15 minutes until flour is medium brown in color; add celery, onion, green pepper, garlic, and tomatoes, and cook them for 8 minutes until they are tender; stir in the thyme, cayenne, bay leaves, fileé, Worcestershire sauce, and stock, making sure nothing is stuck to the bottom of the pot. 3. Stop the process and add the sausage to the pot. 4. Close the lid, turn the pressure release valve to SEAL position, and then move the slider to PRESSURE. Select HI and set the cooking time to 8 minutes. Press START/STOP to begin cooking. When finished, release the pressure quickly. 5. Stir in prawns, salt, and black pepper, and then cook them at Lo3 on SEAR/SAUTÉ mode for 8 minutes or until prawns are cooked through. Discard bay leaves. 6. Serve hot over rice.
**Per Serving:** Calories 393; Fat: 19.86g; Sodium: 1421mg; Carbs: 30.81g; Fibre: 5.2g; Sugar: 4.22g; Protein: 26.34g

## Chipotle Salmon

**Prep Time:** 20 minutes | **Cook Time:** 5 minutes | **Serves:** 3-4

240 ml water
¾ tsp. sea salt, divided
½ tsp. chipotle chili powder
1 tsp. ground cumin
3 to 4 (140-g) salmon fillets with skin, about 2.5 cm thick
Juice of 2 limes
1 tbsp. white vinegar
120 ml avocado oil or olive oil
1 chipotle pepper in adobo sauce
1 tbsp. adobo sauce
10 g chopped fresh coriander
Cooked rice or cauliflower rice, for serving

1. Pour the water into the pot and insert the rack. 2. In a small bowl, combine ¼ teaspoon of the salt and the chipotle chili powder and cumin. 3. Season the salmon with the spice mixture, rubbing it onto the fillets. Place the salmon on the rack with skin side down. 4. Close the lid, turn the pressure release valve to SEAL position, and then move the slider to PRESSURE. Select HI and set the cooking time to 4 minutes. Press START/STOP to begin cooking. When finished, release the pressure quickly. 5. In a blender or food processor, combine the lime juice, vinegar, oil, chipotle pepper, adobo sauce, coriander and remaining ½ teaspoon of salt and blend until smooth. Set aside. 6. Serve the salmon over a bed of rice or cauliflower rice and pour the vinaigrette on top.

**Per Serving:** Calories 330; Fat: 29.9g; Sodium: 493mg; Carbs: 3.7g; Fibre: 0.5g; Sugar: 1.18g; Protein: 13.45g

## Coconut Prawns

**Prep Time:** 10 minutes | **Cook Time:** 10 minutes | **Serves:** 4

240 ml full-fat coconut milk
2 tablespoons freshly squeezed lime juice
1 tablespoon Sriracha
1 red pepper , seeded and chopped
½ teaspoon fine sea salt
Freshly ground black pepper
1 small head cauliflower, cut into florets
455 g fresh or frozen raw prawns, peeled and deveined
200 g sugar snap peas
20 g lightly packed chopped fresh coriander
Lime wedges, for serving

1. Combine the coconut milk, lime juice, Sriracha, pepper , salt, and several grinds of pepper in the pot. 2. Place the rack in the pot and arrange the cauliflower on it. 3. Close the lid, turn the pressure release valve to SEAL position, and then move the slider to PRESSURE. Select HI and set the cooking time to 1 minute. Press START/STOP to begin cooking. When finished, release the pressure quickly. 4. Lift the rack of cauliflower out of the pot. 5. Add the prawns and snap peas to the pot, stir them well, and then simmer them at Lo2 on SEAR/SAUTÉ mode for 3 minutes until they are cooked through with a pink exterior (5 to 6 minutes for frozen). 6. Transfer the cooked cauliflower to a large bowl and use a potato masher to break up the florets into ricelike pieces. 7. Add the coriander to the pot, then ladle the prawns and vegetables over the cauliflower "rice." 8. Serve with lime wedges on the side.

**Per Serving:** Calories 337; Fat: 18.95g; Sodium: 397mg; Carbs: 38.84g; Fibre: 4.4g; Sugar: 29.78g; Protein: 8.06g

## Red Curry Prawns

**Prep Time:** 20 minutes | **Cook Time:** 15 minutes | **Serves:** 6

1 (400-ml) can plus 60 ml coconut milk, divided
1 tsp. ground cumin
1 tsp. paprika
2 tsp. curry powder
3 tbsp fresh lime juice
1½ tsp sea salt, divided, plus more to taste
1 tbsp grated fresh ginger, divided
3 cloves garlic, minced, divided
905 g large prawns, peeled and deveined
2 tbsp coconut oil or olive oil
1 small white onion, diced
1 (800-g) can diced tomatoes
3 tbsp Thai red curry paste
15 g chopped fresh coriander, for garnish (optional)
745 g cooked rice or 440 g cauliflower rice, for serving

1. In a large bowl, combine 60 ml coconut milk and the cumin, paprika, curry powder, lime juice, ½ teaspoon of the salt, 1 teaspoon of the ginger and ⅓ of the garlic, and then add the prawns. Toss to coat and let sit while you prepare the sauce. 2. Select SEAR/SAUTÉ. Select Lo3, and then press START/STOP to begin cooking. 3. Once hot, coat the bottom of the pot with the coconut oil; add onion, remaining ginger and remaining garlic, and sauté them for a few minutes. 4. Stop the process, and add tomatoes, curry paste, the remaining 13.125 g of coconut milk and the remaining teaspoon of salt to the pot. 5. Close the lid, turn the pressure release valve to SEAL position, and then move the slider to PRESSURE. Select HI and set the cooking time to 7 minutes. Press START/STOP to begin cooking. When finished, release the pressure quickly. 6. Toss in the prawns, plus its marinade, and then simmer them at Lo2 on SEAR/SAUTÉ mode for 2 to 5 minutes. 7. Garnish the dish with chopped fresh coriander (optional) and salt to taste, and serve over rice or cauliflower rice.

**Per Serving:** Calories 255; Fat: 9.73g; Sodium: 1644mg; Carbs: 17.84g; Fibre: 7.1g; Sugar: 9.57g; Protein: 26.32g

## Cocktail Prawns

**Prep Time:** 20 minutes | **Cook Time:** 1 minute | **Serves:** 1

240 ml water
½ teaspoon salt
220 g frozen peeled and deveined jumbo prawns
2 tablespoons cocktail sauce
½ medium lemon

1. Add water, salt, and prawns to the pot. 2. Close the lid, turn the pressure release valve to SEAL position, and then move the slider to PRESSURE. 3. Cook the prawns at HI for 0 minute. When finished, release the pressure quickly. 4. Drain prawns. Place prawns in an ice bath 5 minutes to halt the cooking process. 5. Remove to a serving bowl and serve with cocktail sauce and lemon.

**Per Serving:** Calories 209; Fat: 1.28g; Sodium: 1691mg; Carbs: 4.08g; Fibre: 0.7g; Sugar: 2.02g; Protein: 46.23g

# Thai Curry Salmon

**Prep Time:** 10 minutes | **Cook Time:** 15 minutes | **Serves:** 4

| | |
|---|---|
| 1 tablespoon extra-virgin olive oil | 1 tablespoon soy sauce (or tamari, to make it gluten-free) |
| ½ red onion, chopped | 455 g wild-caught Alaskan salmon |
| 1 tablespoon minced fresh ginger (about 2.5 cm knob) | ½ teaspoon fine sea salt |
| 1 tablespoon curry powder | Freshly ground black pepper |
| 1 red pepper, seeded and chopped | 10 g chopped fresh basil |
| One can full-fat coconut milk | 140 g cauliflower "rice" |
| 2 tablespoons pure maple syrup | Chopped fresh coriander or basil, for garnish |
| 1 tablespoon freshly squeezed lime juice | |

1. Add the oil to the pot. Select SEAR/SAUTÉ. Select Lo3, and then press START/STOP to begin cooking. 2. When the oil is hot, add the red onion and sauté for 3 minutes until softened; add ginger and curry powder and stir them for 1 minute more. 3. Stop the process. 4. Add a splash of water to the pan, scraping the bottom with the wooden spoon or a spatula to make sure nothing is stuck. 5. Add the pepper, coconut milk, maple syrup, lime juice, and soy sauce. Arrange the rack on top of the curry and place the salmon on top of the rack in a single layer, skin side down. Sprinkle the salt and a few grinds of pepper over the fish. 6. Close the lid, turn the pressure release valve to SEAL position, and then move the slider to PRESSURE. Select HI and set the cooking time to 2 minutes. Press START/STOP to begin cooking. When finished, release the pressure quickly. 7. Flake the cooked fish directly into the sauce below. The skin will most likely stick to the rack, making it easy to flake the part you want to eat. Remove any small bones you see. Lift the rack out of the pot. 8. Simmer the sauce at Lo2 on SEAR/SAUTÉ mode for 3 minutes until the sauce reduces slightly. 9. Stir in the basil and riced cauliflower, and then stop the process. 10. Serve the curry warm with coriander sprinkled over the top. You can store the leftovers in an airtight container in the fridge for 3 days.

**Per Serving:** Calories 745; Fat: 29.41g; Sodium: 441mg; Carbs: 107.64g; Fibre: 12.9g; Sugar: 16.56g; Protein: 22.19g

## Soy Salmon with Broccoli

**Prep Time:** 5 minutes | **Cook Time:** 5 minutes | **Serves:** 4

455 g wild-caught Alaskan salmon, cut into four 100 g fillets
**Soy-Ginger Dressing:**
6 tablespoons extra-virgin olive oil
2 tablespoons soy sauce or tamari
2 tablespoons raw apple cider vinegar
1 tablespoon minced fresh ginger (about 2.5 cm knob)
1 clove garlic
3 tablespoons pure maple syrup
Fine sea salt and freshly ground black pepper
1 teaspoon toasted sesame oil
455 g broccoli, cut into florets
Sesame seeds, for garnish
Chopped green onions, tender white and green parts only, for garnish

1. 240 ml water into the pot and arrange the rack on the bottom. Place the salmon fillets on the rack in a single layer with skin side down. Sprinkle them generously with salt and pepper. 2. Close the lid, turn the pressure release valve to SEAL position, and then move the slider to PRESSURE. Select HI and set the cooking time to 1 minute. Press START/STOP to begin cooking. When finished, release the pressure naturally. 3. Remove the lid and place the broccoli directly on top of the cooked fish, and then cook them at HI on PRESSURE COOK for 0 minute. Release the steam pressure quickly. 4. Remove the lid and place the broccoli directly on top of the cooked fish, and then cook them at HI on PRESSURE COOK for 0 minute. Release the steam pressure quickly. 5. Transfer the steamed broccoli and salmon to serving plates. 6. Combine the olive oil, soy sauce, vinegar, ginger, garlic, maple syrup, and sesame oil in a blender and blend them for 1 minute until smooth. 7. Drizzle the dressing over the top and garnish with the sesame seeds and green onions. 8. You can store the leftovers in an airtight container in the fridge for 4 days.

**Per Serving:** Calories 207; Fat: 12.22g; Sodium: 341mg; Carbs: 21.17g; Fibre: 3.7g; Sugar: 11.28g; Protein: 5.37g

## Celery Tuna Noodle Casserole

**Prep Time:** 5 minutes | **Cook Time:** 5 minutes | **Serves:** 6

| | |
|---|---|
| 480 ml chicken stock | ¼ teaspoon table salt |
| 240 ml regular or low-fat evaporated milk | 300 g wide egg or no-yolk noodles |
| 100 g white button mushrooms, thinly sliced | 240 g heavy cream |
| 2 medium celery stalks, thinly sliced | Two 150 g cans tuna, preferably yellow fin tuna packed in oil, drained |
| 2 tablespoons butter | |
| 1 teaspoon onion powder | 200 g grated Swiss cheese |
| 1 teaspoon ground dried mustard | |

1. Mix the stock, evaporated milk, mushrooms, celery, butter, onion powder, dried mustard, and salt in the pot. Stir in the noodles until well coated. 2. Close the lid, turn the pressure release valve to SEAL position, and then move the slider to PRESSURE. Select HI and set the cooking time to 4 minutes. Press START/STOP to begin cooking. When finished, release the pressure quickly. 3. Stir in the cream, and then cook them at Lo3 on SEAR/SAUTÉ mode for 1 minute until the sauce is bubbling fairly well. 4. Stop the process, and gently stir in the tuna and cheese. Set the lid askew over the unit for a couple of minutes to melt the cheese. 5. Serve and enjoy.

**Per Serving:** Calories 537; Fat: 36.95g; Sodium: 798mg; Carbs: 7.99g; Fibre: 0.7g; Sugar: 3.26g; Protein: 42.44g

## Quick Prawns Boil

**Prep Time:** 5 minutes | **Cook Time:** 15 minutes | **Serves:** 4

| | |
|---|---|
| 240 ml chicken stock | ½ tablespoon Old Bay seasoning |
| 1 teaspoon minced garlic | 110 g peeled and deveined extra-large prawns |
| 2 medium red potatoes, quartered | 3 tablespoons butter, melted |
| 1 medium ear corn, husked | ½ medium lemon, for serving |
| 1 (75 g) link andouille sausage, cut into 4 pieces on the bias | 1 tablespoon chopped fresh parsley |

1. Add stock and garlic to the pot and then place in the rack. 2. Add potatoes, corn, and sausage, and then sprinkle Old Bay seasoning over everything. 3. Close the lid, turn the pressure release valve to SEAL position, and then move the slider to PRESSURE. Select HI and set the cooking time to 3 minutes. Press START/STOP to begin cooking. When finished, release the pressure quickly. 4. Add prawns, stir, then immediately replace the lid and wait for 5 to 8 minutes until the prawns is pink and cooked through. 5. To serve, remove everything to a large bowl and serve with a side of butter, lemon, and sprinkle of parsley.

**Per Serving:** Calories 398; Fat: 18.34g; Sodium: 688mg; Carbs: 40.89g; Fibre: 5.3g; Sugar: 3.7g; Protein: 20.13g

## Garlic-Chili Fish Tacos

**Prep Time:** 15 minutes | **Cook Time:** 5 minutes | **Serves:** 4

½ tablespoon olive oil
½ teaspoon minced garlic
⅛ teaspoon smoked paprika
⅛ teaspoon chili powder
⅛ teaspoon ground cumin
**Spicy Lime Crema:**
2 tablespoons sour cream
1 tablespoon mayonnaise
1 teaspoon lime juice
**For Serving:**
3 small tortillas, warmed
30 g shredded cabbage
1 ½ tablespoons pico de gallo

¼ teaspoon salt
⅛ teaspoon Cajun seasoning
2 (110 g) frozen tilapia fillets
240 ml water

⅛ teaspoon garlic salt
⅛ teaspoon salt
½ teaspoon sriracha sauce

1 tablespoon chopped coriander
½ medium lime

1. Mix together oil and all the spices in a small bowl, and then spread evenly over both sides of fillets. 2. Pour water into the pot and place in the rack. Place fish on rack. 3. Close the lid, turn the pressure release valve to SEAL position, and then move the slider to PRESSURE. Select HI and set the cooking time to 2 minutes. Press START/STOP to begin cooking. When finished, release the pressure quickly. 4. Carefully transfer fish to a small bowl. 5. In a separate small bowl, combine all Spicy Lime Crema ingredients and refrigerate until ready to use. 6. To serve, transfer tortillas to a serving plate. Evenly break up the fish between tortillas. Top the dish with cabbage, pico de gallo, Spicy Lime Crema, coriander, and a squeeze of lime.
**Per Serving:** Calories 209; Fat: 7.42g; Sodium: 584mg; Carbs: 31.21g; Fibre: 1.2g; Sugar: 11.8g; Protein: 4.92g

## Honey-Garlic Salmon

**Prep Time:** 5 minutes | **Cook Time:** 15 minutes | **Serves:** 2

60 ml soy sauce
2 tablespoons honey
½ tablespoon apple cider vinegar
½ tablespoon olive oil

1 ½ tablespoons brown sugar
½ teaspoon minced garlic
1 (125 g) frozen salmon fillet

1. Stir all of the ingredients together in the pot. 2. Close the lid, turn the pressure release valve to SEAL position, and then move the slider to PRESSURE. Select HI and set the cooking time to 3 minutes. Press START/STOP to begin cooking. When finished, release the pressure naturally. 3. Transfer the fish to a plate or bowl. 4. Cook the sauce at Hi5 on SEAR/SAUTÉ mode for 8 minutes until reduced and thickened. 5. Spoon 1 tablespoon sauce over fish and serve.
**Per Serving:** Calories 311; Fat: 14.26g; Sodium: 791mg; Carbs: 29.29g; Fibre: 0.7g; Sugar: 27.12g; Protein: 17.01g

## Pesto Tilapia with Sun-Dried Tomatoes

**Prep Time:** 5 minutes | **Cook Time:** 5 minutes | **Serves:** 2

| | |
|---|---|
| 1 tablespoon butter | 120 ml chicken stock |
| 3 tablespoons chopped sun-dried tomatoes | 1 tablespoon basil pesto |
| 55 g artichoke heart quarters | 2 (110g) frozen tilapia fillets |
| 1 teaspoon lemon juice | 2 tablespoons heavy cream |
| ⅛ teaspoon salt | 3 tablespoons shredded Parmesan cheese |
| ⅛ teaspoon ground black pepper | |

1. Add butter, tomatoes, artichokes, lemon juice, salt, pepper, and stock to the pot. 2. Spread pesto all over the tops of fillets and place on the rack. Lower the rack into the pot. 3. Close the lid, turn the pressure release valve to SEAL position, and then move the slider to PRESSURE. Select HI and set the cooking time to 2 minutes. Press START/STOP to begin cooking. When finished, release the pressure quickly. 4. Carefully transfer fish to a serving plate. 5. Stir cream and Parmesan into the sauce. Ladle sauce over fish and serve.

**Per Serving:** Calories 387; Fat: 21.3g; Sodium: 701mg; Carbs: 30.64g; Fibre: 2.9g; Sugar: 22.45g; Protein: 20.55g

## Old Bay-Seasoned Lobster Tails

**Prep Time:** 10 minutes | **Cook Time:** 0 minute | **Serves:** 2

| | |
|---|---|
| 2 (150 g) lobster tails | ½ teaspoon salt |
| ⅛ teaspoon Old Bay seasoning | ½ teaspoon chopped parsley |
| 240 ml water | 2 tablespoons clarified butter |
| ½ teaspoon minced garlic | 2 lemon wedges |

1. Cut down the centre of each lobster tail all the way to the base of the tail. 2. Carefully crack open the lobster to expose the meat underneath, and then slide your finger on the underside of the meat to loosen it from the bottom of the shell. 3. Pop the meat up and above the shell so it lies gently on the outer shell but is still connected to the tail. Sprinkle the lobster tails with Old Bay seasoning, then set aside. 4. Add water, garlic, and salt to the pot, then place in the rack and place the lobsters on it. 5. Close the lid, turn the pressure release valve to SEAL position, and then move the slider to PRESSURE. Select LO and set the cooking time to 0 minute. Press START/STOP to begin cooking. When finished, release the pressure naturally. 6. Take the internal temperature of lobster. It should be 60°C. If it is a little under, replace the lid and wait 2 minutes before checking again. Lobster is extremely delicate and easy to overcook. 7. Remove lobster tails to a plate and top with parsley. Serve the dish with butter and lemon.

**Per Serving:** Calories 229; Fat: 12.77g; Sodium: 1310mg; Carbs: 3.61g; Fibre: 0.2g; Sugar: 1.23g; Protein: 25.13g

## Brown Butter Pasta with Scallops & Tomatoes

**Prep Time:** 5 minutes | **Cook Time:** 6 minutes | **Serves:** 4

240 ml chicken stock
1 teaspoon minced garlic
⅛ teaspoon crushed red pepper flakes
80 g uncooked angel hair pasta, broken in half
75 g frozen bay scallops
2 tablespoons brown butter
50 g halved cherry tomatoes
2 tablespoons heavy cream
1 tablespoon minced fresh parsley

1. Add stock, garlic, and red pepper flakes. Layer pasta in a crisscross pattern over the liquid to reduce clumping. 2. Close the lid, turn the pressure release valve to SEAL position, and then move the slider to PRESSURE. Select HI and set the cooking time to 1 minute. Press START/STOP to begin cooking. When finished, release the pressure quickly. 3. Immediately stir in scallops, brown butter, tomatoes, and cream, and stir them for 5 minutes until scallops are completely cooked through. 4. Transfer the dish to a serving dish and top with parsley. Serve.

**Per Serving:** Calories 225; Fat: 13.02g; Sodium: 407mg; Carbs: 9.04g; Fibre: 1.3g; Sugar: 0.39g; Protein: 17.36g

## Scallop Risotto with Spinach

**Prep Time:** 5 minutes | **Cook Time:** 35 minutes | **Serves:** 2

75 g frozen bay scallops
⅛ teaspoon salt
⅛ teaspoon ground black pepper
2 tablespoons butter, divided
½ tablespoon dried onion flakes
½ teaspoon minced garlic
100 g uncooked Arborio rice
240 ml chicken stock
1 tablespoon white wine
1 ½ tablespoons lemon juice
15 g packed spinach

1. Season the scallops with salt and pepper. 2. Select SEAR/SAUTÉ. Select Hi5, and then press START/STOP to begin cooking. 3. Add 1 tablespoon butter to the pot and swirl for about 3 minutes until browned. Add scallops and stir them for about 3 to 5 minutes until fully cooked. Remove them to a serving plate. 4. Add remaining 1 tablespoon butter, onion flakes, garlic, and rice, and stir them for 2 to 3 minutes to toast the rice. 5. Add stock, wine, and lemon juice and deglaze the pot, scraping all the browned bits off the bottom of the pot. Stop the process. 6. Close the lid, turn the pressure release valve to SEAL position, and then move the slider to PRESSURE. Select HI and set the cooking time to 10 minutes. Press START/STOP to begin cooking. When finished, release the pressure naturally. 7. Stir spinach into risotto about 3 minutes until wilted. Stir in scallops and brown butter right before serving. 8. Transfer them to a serving plate and serve immediately.

**Per Serving:** Calories 435; Fat: 26.32g; Sodium: 971mg; Carbs: 20.09g; Fibre: 6.6g; Sugar: 1.3g; Protein: 37.34g

## Salmon with Zesty Dill Sauce

**Prep Time:** 5 minutes | **Cook Time:** 5 minutes | **Serves:** 4

60 ml water
60 ml lemon juice
2 sprigs fresh dill
1 (200 g) skinless salmon fillet
**Zesty Dill Sauce:**
1 ½ tablespoons sour cream
1 ½ tablespoons mayonnaise
½ teaspoon minced fresh dill
¼ teaspoon Dijon mustard
¼ teaspoon salt
¼ teaspoon ground black pepper
3 slices lemon

¼ teaspoon lemon zest
½ tablespoon lemon juice
⅛ teaspoon garlic salt

1. Add water, lemon juice, and fresh dill to the pot, and place in the rack. 2. Sprinkle salmon with salt and pepper on all sides, then place lemon slices on top of salmon. Place salmon on the rack. 3. Close the lid, turn the pressure release valve to SEAL position, and then move the slider to PRESSURE. Select HI and set the cooking time to 5 minutes. Press START/STOP to begin cooking. When finished, release the pressure naturally. 4. While the fish cooks, prepare the Zesty Dill Sauce. In a small bowl, combine all sauce ingredients and refrigerate until ready to use. 5. Transfer salmon to a plate and serve immediately with dill sauce.

**Per Serving:** Calories 125; Fat: 6.52g; Sodium: 443mg; Carbs: 4.66g; Fibre: 0.3g; Sugar: 1.55g; Protein: 12.5g

## Crab Legs with Lemon Wedges

**Prep Time:** 5 minutes | **Cook Time:** 1 minute | **Serves:** 2

240 ml water
455 g crab legs
⅛ teaspoon Old Bay seasoning
2 tablespoons clarified butter
½ medium lemon cut into wedges

1. Pour water into pot and place in the rack. 2. Add crab legs and sprinkle with Old Bay seasoning. 3. Close the lid, turn the pressure release valve to SEAL position, and then move the slider to PRESSURE. Select LO and set the cooking time to 1 minute. Press START/STOP to begin cooking. When finished, release the pressure quickly. 4. Remove crab to a plate and serve with butter and lemon.

**Per Serving:** Calories 302; Fat: 14g; Sodium: 758mg; Carbs: 0.96g; Fibre: 0g; Sugar: 0.31g; Protein: 41.13g

# Chapter 6 Beef, Pork and Lamb

## Mongolian Beef

**Prep Time:** 5 minutes | **Cook Time:** 15 minutes | **Serves:** 4

455 g skirt steak
80 ml soy sauce (or tamari, to make it gluten-free)
3 tablespoons pure maple syrup
1 tablespoon raw apple cider vinegar
1 tablespoon minced fresh ginger (2.5 cm knob)
2 cloves garlic, minced
125 g sliced shiitake mushrooms
190 g bulgur (or white rice, to make it gluten-free)
300 ml plus 2 tablespoons water
2 heads baby bok choy
120 g sugar snap peas
120 g shredded carrots
1 tablespoon cornflour
60 g chopped green onions, tender white and green parts only
Chopped fresh coriander, for garnish
Sesame seeds, for garnish

1. Thinly cut the steak across the grain into 1 cm-thick slices. 2. Place the steak in the pot and add the soy sauce, maple syrup, vinegar, ginger, garlic, and mushrooms. Stir to coat the beef. 3. In an oven-safe bowl, combine the bulgur and 300 ml of the water. Arrange the rack over the meat and place the bowl on top. 4. Close the lid, turn the pressure release valve to SEAL position, and then move the slider to PRESSURE. Select HI and set the cooking time to 4 minutes. Press START/STOP to begin cooking. When finished, release the pressure naturally. 5. To prepare the bok choy, trim the ends, rinse well to remove any dirt, then slice crosswise into 2.5 cm pieces. 6. Lift the rack and the bowl out of the pot, then add the bok choy, snap peas, and carrots to the pot, and cook them at Lo3 on SEAR/SAUTÉ mode for 5 minutes until the vegetables are crisp-tender. 7. In a separate bowl, stir together the cornflour and the 2 tablespoons water to make slurry. Pour the slurry into the pot and stir for 1 to 2 minutes until the sauce thickens. 8. Serve the beef and vegetables over the cooked bulgur with a generous topping of green onions, coriander, and sesame seeds. 9. You can store the leftovers in an airtight container in the fridge for 3 or 4 days.

**Per Serving:** Calories 513; Fat: 12.1g; Sodium: 1820mg; Carbs: 62.55g; Fibre: 4.4g; Sugar: 12.54g; Protein: 39.24g

## Cheese Sandwiches

**Prep Time:** 20 minutes | **Cook Time:** 10 minutes | **Serves:** 6

2 tsp olive oil
1 (905-g) chuck roast
Coarse salt
Freshly ground black pepper
2 medium onions, sliced

475 ml beef stock
2 sprigs thyme
6 crusty rolls split, buttered and toasted
6 slices Swiss cheese
Dijon mustard

1. Season the chuck roast well with salt and pepper. 2. Select SEAR/SAUTÉ. Select Lo3, and then press START/STOP to begin cooking. 3. When hot, add the oil to the pot, and then brown the roast well on all sides. Transfer the roast to a plate and set aside. 4. Add the onions to the drippings in the pot and scrape up any browned bits on the bottom of the pot; sauté the onions for 10 minutes until they are soft and starting to caramelize. 5. Add the beef stock to the pot, taking care to scrape up any browned bits from the bottom of the pot. Place the roast and thyme sprigs directly into the liquid. Stop the process. 6. Close the lid, turn the pressure release valve to SEAL position, and then move the slider to PRESSURE. Select HI and set the cooking time to 40 minutes. Press START/STOP to begin cooking. When finished, release the pressure naturally. 7. Divide the meat among the roll bottoms and top each with a slice of Swiss cheese. Spread Dijon on the underside of the roll tops and place over the cheese.

**Per Serving:** Calories 451; Fat: 19.76g; Sodium: 1725mg; Carbs: 25.66g; Fibre: 1.5g; Sugar: 4.43g; Protein: 40.86g

## Herbed Pork Loin

**Prep Time:** 20 minutes | **Cook Time:** 15 minutes | **Serves:** 4

2 tsp olive oil
3 cloves garlic, minced
2 tsp Italian seasoning
1 tsp. coarse salt

½ tsp. freshly ground black pepper
680 g pork tenderloin
240 ml water or chicken stock

1. Mix the olive oil, garlic, Italian seasoning, salt and pepper in a small bowl. Rub the mixture all over the outside of the pork loin. 2. Pour the water or stock into the pot and insert the rack. Place the pork loin on the rack. 3. Close the lid, turn the pressure release valve to SEAL position, and then move the slider to PRESSURE. Select HI and set the cooking time to 25 minutes. Press START/STOP to begin cooking. When finished, release the pressure naturally. 4. Remove the pork and allow it to rest on a carving board for 5 minutes, then slice and serve.

**Per Serving:** Calories 289; Fat: 8.63g; Sodium: 893mg; Carbs: 4.51g; Fibre: 0.4g; Sugar: 0.3g; Protein: 45.28g

## Gravy Pork Chops with Onion

**Prep Time:** 20 minutes | **Cook Time:** 25 minutes | **Serves:** 4

4 (2.5-cm thick) bone-in pork chops
Coarse salt
Freshly ground pepper
2 tsp olive oil
1 large onion, sliced
240 ml beef stock
60 ml heavy cream
1 tbsp cornflour

1. Season the chops with salt and pepper. 2. Select SEAR/SAUTÉ. Select Lo3, and then press START/STOP to begin cooking. 3. When hot, add the olive oil, and then brown the chops for 5 minutes on both sides. Transfer the chops to a plate and set them aside. 4. Add the onion to the pot and cook for 5 minutes until the onion is starting to soften; add the beef stock, stirring to scrape up any browned bits from the bottom of the pot. Return the pork chops to the pot. 5. Close the lid, turn the pressure release valve to SEAL position, and then move the slider to PRESSURE. Select HI and set the cooking time to 10 minutes. Press START/STOP to begin cooking. When finished, release the pressure naturally. 6. Remove the chops and tent with foil to keep warm. 7. In a small bowl, mix together the cream and cornflour, then pour into the pot. Stir for 2 to 3 minutes until the sauce is thickened. Pour the sauce over the pork chops and serve.

**Per Serving:** Calories 426; Fat: 24.9g; Sodium: 245mg; Carbs: 6.78g; Fibre: 1g; Sugar: 2.42g; Protein: 41.49g

## Pork Ragù

**Prep Time:** 5 minutes | **Cook Time:** 15 minutes | **Serves:** 4

900 g boneless pork shoulder, cut into 5 cm pieces and any large chunks of fat removed
900 g plum or Roma tomatoes, chopped
240 ml chicken stock
1 small yellow onion, chopped
2 medium celery stalks, thinly sliced
2 tablespoons fresh oregano leaves, finely chopped
2 tablespoons fresh rosemary leaves, finely chopped
½ teaspoon table salt
½ teaspoon ground black pepper
60 g heavy cream
10 g loosely packed parsley leaves, chopped

1. Mix the pork, tomatoes, stock, onion, celery, oregano, rosemary, salt, and pepper in the pot. 2. Close the lid, turn the pressure release valve to SEAL position, and then move the slider to PRESSURE. Select HI and set the cooking time to 45 minutes. Press START/STOP to begin cooking. When finished, release the pressure naturally. 3. Use a flatware tablespoon to skim any excess surface fat from the top of the sauce. Break up the pork pieces into smaller bits and shreds, stirring these into the sauce. 4. Bring the sauce to a simmer at Lo2 on SEAR/SAUTÉ mode, stir in the cream and cook them for 4 minutes until somewhat thickened. 5. Transfer the food to the serving plate and stir in the parsley. Enjoy.

**Per Serving:** Calories 625; Fat: 15.01g; Sodium: 716mg; Carbs: 56.56g; Fibre: 3g; Sugar: 52g; Protein: 65.61g

## Mexican Beef Casserole

**Prep Time:** 20 minutes | **Cook Time:** 15 minutes | **Serves:** 4

| | |
|---|---|
| 2 tsp olive oil | 1 red pepper, seeded and chopped |
| 1 medium onion, chopped | 1 poblano pepper, chopped |
| 3 cloves garlic, minced | 1 jalapeño pepper, minced |
| 455 g beef mince | 1 (455-g) jar red salsa |
| 1 tbsp chipotle chili powder | 1 (410-g) can fire-roasted diced tomatoes |
| 1 tbsp ancho chili powder | 220 g Mexican-blend shredded cheese |
| 1 tbsp ground cumin | 2 green onions, chopped |
| 120 ml water | 10 g chopped fresh coriander |
| 195 g uncooked long-grain white rice | |

1. Select SEAR/SAUTÉ. Select Lo3, and then press START/STOP to begin cooking. 2. When hot, add olive oil and onion, and then cook them for 5 minutes until the onion is soft; add garlic, beef mince, chili powders and cumin, and cook the beef until no pink remains. 3. Add the water, taking care to scrape up any browned bits from the bottom of the pot. 4. Stop the process, and add the rice, the bell, poblano and jalapeño peppers, and the salsa and tomatoes in order without stirring. 5. Close the lid, turn the pressure release valve to SEAL position, and then move the slider to PRESSURE. Select HI and set the cooking time to 9 minutes. Press START/STOP to begin cooking. When finished, release the pressure naturally. 6. Stir in the cheese, and then top with green onions and coriander.

**Per Serving:** Calories 704; Fat: 32.59g; Sodium: 514mg; Carbs: 52.89g; Fibre: 5.9g; Sugar: 8.17g; Protein: 49.8g

## Round Roast with Veggies

**Prep Time:** 15 minutes | **Cook Time:** 25 minutes | **Serves:** 6

| | |
|---|---|
| 1.1 kg round roast (top or bottom) | ½ tsp. ground black pepper |
| 2 tbsp. olive oil | 1 tbsp. thyme |
| 480 ml vegetable or beef stock | 200 – 300 g sliced mushrooms |
| 2 tbsp. minced garlic | 1 large white onion, sliced or diced |
| 1 tsp. salt | 455 g potatoes, quartered or cubed |

1. Mix the olive oil, stock, garlic, salt, pepper, and thyme in the pot. Add the roast, mushrooms, and onion, and stir them well. 2. Close the lid, turn the pressure release valve to SEAL position, and then move the slider to PRESSURE. Select HI and set the cooking time to 25 minutes. Press START/STOP to begin cooking. When finished, release the pressure quickly. 3. Serve.

**Per Serving:** Calories 484; Fat: 14.34g; Sodium: 943mg; Carbs: 25.79g; Fibre: 3.4g; Sugar: 3.26g; Protein: 60.2g

## Carrot Lamb Ragù

**Prep Time:** 20 minutes | **Cook Time:** 15 minutes | **Serves:** 2

3 tablespoons olive oil
1 large yellow onion, chopped
2 medium carrots, chopped
4 medium garlic cloves, peeled and minced
675 g boneless leg of lamb, cut into 5 cm pieces
240 ml chicken stock
2 tablespoons fresh rosemary leaves, chopped
2 tablespoons fresh sage leaves, chopped
½ teaspoon table salt
½ teaspoon ground black pepper
1 (150 g) can tomato paste

1. Select SEAR/SAUTÉ. Select Lo3, and then press START/STOP to begin cooking. 2. When hot, heat the oil for 1 to 2 minutes; add onion and carrot, and cook them for 5 minutes until the onion begins to soften; stir in the garlic and cook for a few seconds; add the lamb pieces and stir them for 1 minute just until the lamb is thoroughly mixed into the vegetables. 3. Stop the process, and stir in the stock, rosemary, sage, salt, and pepper. 4. Close the lid, turn the pressure release valve to SEAL position, and then move the slider to PRESSURE. Select HI and set the cooking time to 30 minutes. Press START/STOP to begin cooking. When finished, release the pressure naturally. 5. Break up the meat into smaller pieces. Stir in the tomato paste until uniform. 6. Bring the sauce to a simmer at Lo2 on SEAR/SAUTÉ mode for 5 minutes until thickened. 7. Set the lid askew over the pot for 5 minutes to blend the flavors. 8. Serve and enjoy.

**Per Serving:** Calories 1012; Fat: 53.39g; Sodium: 1448mg; Carbs: 30.88g; Fibre: 7.3g; Sugar: 15.83g; Protein: 101.14g

## Feta Beef with Olives

**Prep Time:** 15 minutes | **Cook Time:** 45 minutes | **Serves:** 4-6

900 g beef stew meat, cubed (5 cm)
1 tbsp. olive oil
720 g spicy diced tomatoes with juice
60 g green olives, drained
60 g black olives, drained
½ tsp. salt
120 g feta cheese

1. Select SEAR/SAUTÉ. Select Lo3, and then press START/STOP to begin cooking. 2. When hot, heat the oil and sauté the beef until light brown. 3. Stir in the tomatoes, green and black olives, and salt, and then stop the process. 4. Close the lid, turn the pressure release valve to SEAL position, and then move the slider to PRESSURE. Select HI and set the cooking time to 45 minutes. Press START/STOP to begin cooking. When finished, release the pressure naturally. 5. Taste and season the dish more if necessary. 6. Add the feta cheese and serve with cooked rice or potatoes.

**Per Serving:** Calories 313; Fat: 15.18g; Sodium: 1042mg; Carbs: 7.75g; Fibre: 1g; Sugar: 5.2g; Protein: 38.14g

## Barbecue Pulled Pork Sandwiches

**Prep Time:** 15 minutes | **Cook Time:** 45 minutes | **Serves:** 2

| | |
|---|---|
| ½ tablespoon packed light brown sugar | ¼ teaspoon freshly ground black pepper |
| ½ teaspoon paprika | 455 g boneless pork shoulder roast |
| ½ teaspoon salt | 1 teaspoon oil |
| ½ teaspoon ground mustard | 120 ml chicken stock |
| ¼ teaspoon ground cumin | 480 g classic barbecue sauce, divided |

1. Combine the brown sugar, paprika, salt, mustard, cumin, and pepper in a small bowl. Rub the mixture all over the pork roast. 2. Select SEAR/SAUTÉ. Select Lo3, and then press START/STOP to begin cooking. 3. When hot, add oil and brown the pork for 2 to 3 minutes per side. 4. Stop the process, then add stock and 240 g of barbecue sauce to the pot and stir them well. 5. Close the lid, turn the pressure release valve to SEAL position, and then move the slider to PRESSURE. Select HI and set the cooking time to 45 minutes. Press START/STOP to begin cooking. When finished, release the pressure naturally. 6. Transfer the pork to a large bowl. Stir the contents of the pot and allow simmering for 10 to 12 minutes, or until thickened and reduced. 7. During cooking, use a spoon to remove any fat that rises to the top. Taste and adjust the seasonings as necessary. 8. Shred the pork with two forks. Return the meat to the pot, stir, and warm through. 9. Serve on hamburger buns or Portobello mushroom caps with additional barbecue sauce and coleslaw.

**Per Serving:** Calories 838; Fat: 14.29g; Sodium: 3716mg; Carbs: 119.3g; Fibre: 2.9g; Sugar: 96.12g; Protein: 54.9g

## Stew Beef and Broccoli

**Prep Time:** 25 minutes | **Cook Time:** 35 minutes | **Serves:** 4

| | |
|---|---|
| 455 g stew beef meat | 120 ml beef or bone stock |
| 1 onion, quartered | 60 ml soy sauce |
| 1 clove garlic, large-sized, pressed | 2 tbsp. fish sauce |
| 1 tsp. ground ginger | 1 bag (250 g- 300 g) frozen broccoli |
| ½ tsp. salt | |

1. Mix the beef meat, onion, garlic, ginger and salt in the pot. 2. Pour the stock, soy sauce and fish sauce into the pot, stir them well. 3. Close the lid, turn the pressure release valve to SEAL position, and then move the slider to PRESSURE. Select HI and set the cooking time to 35 minutes. Press START/STOP to begin cooking. When finished, release the pressure naturally. 4. Add the broccoli, close the lid and let sit for 15 minutes. 5. Serve.

**Per Serving:** Calories 435; Fat: 10.22g; Sodium: 1578mg; Carbs: 50.03g; Fibre: 24.6g; Sugar: 16.23g; Protein: 51.38g

# Beef Enchiladas

**Prep Time:** 30 minutes | **Cook Time:** 60 minutes | **Serves:** 2

1 tablespoon oil, plus more for greasing
455 g beef roast
Salt
Freshly ground black pepper
1 small onion, chopped
240 ml beef stock
110 g tomato salsa
1 tablespoon red wine vinegar
½ tablespoon ground cumin
1 (250 g) can enchilada sauce, divided
6 (15 cm) corn or flour tortillas
100 g shredded sharp Cheddar cheese

1. Season the beef with salt and pepper. 2. Select SEAR/SAUTÉ. Select Lo3, and then press START/STOP to begin cooking. 3. When hot, add 1 tablespoon of oil and sear the beef for 8 to 10 minutes on all sides. 4. Stop the process, and add onion, stock, salsa, vinegar, and cumin to the pot. 5. Close the lid, turn the pressure release valve to SEAL position, and then move the slider to PRESSURE. Select HI and set the cooking time to 60 minutes. Press START/STOP to begin cooking. When finished, release the pressure naturally. 6. Transfer the roast from the pot to a large bowl, discarding the liquid. Shred the roast. 7. Add 60 g of the enchilada sauce to the meat and toss to combine. Taste and adjust the seasonings if desired. 8. Coat a suitable baking pan with oil. Spread half of the remaining enchilada sauce (about 120 g on the bottom of the prepared baking pan. 9. Lay the tortillas out on a cutting board. Fill each tortilla with the shredded beef mixture and 1 tablespoon of cheese. Roll up and place seam-side down in the baking dish. Pour the remaining enchilada sauce over the top of the enchiladas and sprinkle with the remaining cheese. 10. Add the baking pan to the pot. Close the lid and move slider to AIR FRY/STOVETOP, then use the dial to select BAKE/ROAST. Adjust the cooking temperature to 175°C and set the cooking time to 20 minutes. Press START/STOP to begin cooking. 11. Transfer the dish to a cooling rack and let rest for 5 to 10 minutes before serving with sour cream, guacamole, salsa, and chopped coriander .

**Per Serving:** Calories 1289; Fat: 62.26g; Sodium: 3062mg; Carbs: 91.8g; Fibre: 8.3g; Sugar: 15g; Protein: 92.39g

## Italian Roast Ragù

**Prep Time:** 15 minutes | **Cook Time:** 60 minutes | **Serves:** 4

| | |
|---|---|
| 2 tablespoons olive oil | 1 medium garlic clove, peeled and minced (1 teaspoon) |
| 900 g boneless beef chuck, trimmed of any large chunks of fat and cut in half | 1 tablespoon dried rosemary |
| 1 can whole tomatoes | 2 teaspoons dried oregano |
| 60 g frozen pearl onions (do not thaw) | 1 bay leaf |
| 180 ml light dry red wine, such as Pinot Noir | ½ teaspoon table salt |
| 1 tablespoon drained and rinsed capers, chopped | ½ teaspoon ground black pepper |

1. Select SEAR/SAUTÉ. Select Lo3, and then press START/STOP to begin cooking. 2. When hot, heat the oil for 1 to 2 minutes, and then brown the beef pieces. Transfer the beef to a bowl. 3. Squeeze the whole tomatoes over the pot, and then add any remaining juice from the can. Add the pearl onions and stir well to scrape up all the browned bits on the bottom of the pot, and cook them for 2 minutes just until the onions begin to brown lightly. 4. Stop the process, and stir in wine, capers, garlic, rosemary, oregano, bay leaf, salt, and pepper, and then return the beef pieces and any juice in the bowl to the pot. 5. Close the lid, turn the pressure release valve to SEAL position, and then move the slider to PRESSURE. Select HI and set the cooking time to 55 minutes. Press START/STOP to begin cooking. When finished, release the pressure naturally. 6. Use a flatware tablespoon to skim off any excess surface fat. Find and discard the bay leaf, then use two forks to shred the meat. 7. Bring the sauce to a full simmer at Lo2 on SEAR/SAUTÉ mode for 5 minutes until reduced to a fairly wet ragù. 8. Stop the process and set the lid askew over the pot for 5 minutes to blend the flavors.

**Per Serving:** Calories 399; Fat: 19.9g; Sodium: 582mg; Carbs: 9.18g; Fibre: 1.4g; Sugar: 6.19g; Protein: 47.45g

## Mozzarella Pork Chops

**Prep Time:** 20 minutes | **Cook Time:** 10 minutes | **Serves:** 4

| | |
|---|---|
| 4 boneless pork chops | 240 ml water |
| 2 tbsp. olive oil | 4 tbsp. hot sauce |
| ½ tsp. salt or to taste | 4 tbsp. butter |
| ½ tsp. ground black pepper | 120 g mozzarella cheese, grated |

1. Select SEAR/SAUTÉ. Select Lo3, and then press START/STOP to begin cooking. 2. When hot, heat the oil and brown the meat for 3 minutes on both sides. 3. Pour in the water and hot sauce, and place the butter on top of each pork chop, and then stop the process. 4. Close the lid, turn the pressure release valve to SEAL position, and then move the slider to PRESSURE. Select HI and set the cooking time to 10 minutes. Press START/STOP to begin cooking. When finished, release the pressure naturally. 5. Sprinkle the pork chops with mozzarella cheese. Close the lid and let sit for 5 minutes. 6. Serve.

**Per Serving:** Calories 445; Fat: 24.64g; Sodium: 811mg; Carbs: 2.74g; Fibre: 0.9g; Sugar: 1.42g; Protein: 50.92g

## Beef Bow-Ties in Spicy Tomato-Almond Sauce

**Prep Time:** 15 minutes | **Cook Time:** 20 minutes | **Serves:** 4

2 tablespoons vegetable, corn, or rapeseed oil
1 small red onion, halved and sliced into thin half-moons
1 tablespoon minced peeled fresh ginger
455 g beef mince
1 can diced tomatoes
6 tablespoons almond butter
2 tablespoons honey
2 teaspoons mild paprika
1 teaspoon ground cinnamon
1 teaspoon ground cloves
1 teaspoon ground coriander
1 teaspoon ground cumin
1 teaspoon table salt
½ teaspoon cayenne
540 ml chicken stock
200 g dried bow-tie (or farfalle) pasta

1. Select SEAR/SAUTÉ. Select Lo3, and then press START/STOP to begin cooking. 2. When hot, heat the oil for 1 to 2 minutes; add onion and ginger, and cook them for 3 minutes until the onion begins to soften; crumble in the beef mince and cook for 3 minutes, stirring frequently to break up any clumps until the meat loses its raw and pink color. 3. Stir in the tomatoes and almond butter until the almond butter dissolves in the sauce, all the while scraping up every speck of browned stuff on the pot's bottom. 4. Stir in the honey, paprika, cinnamon, cloves, coriander, cumin, salt, and cayenne until uniform. Stop the process. 5. Close the lid, turn the pressure release valve to SEAL position, and then move the slider to PRESSURE. Select HI and set the cooking time to 7 minutes. Press START/STOP to begin cooking. When finished, release the pressure naturally. 6. Stir the dish well before serving.

**Per Serving:** Calories 923; Fat: 47.59g; Sodium: 1350mg; Carbs: 59.25g; Fibre: 7.8g; Sugar: 10.38g; Protein: 64.61g

## Lamb Mince with Black Beans

**Prep Time:** 20 minutes | **Cook Time:** 25 minutes | **Serves:** 4-6

455 g lamb mince
2 tbsp. vegetable oil
60 g chopped onion
½ tsp. salt
1½ tbsp. chili powder
½ tsp. cayenne
2 tsp. cumin
1 can undrained diced tomatoes
1½ tbsp. tomato paste
1 can chopped and undrained green chilies
2 cans drained black beans
360 ml chicken stock

1. Select SEAR/SAUTÉ. Select Lo3, and then press START/STOP to begin cooking. 2. When hot, heat the oil, and add the lamb, onion and salt and sauté for 5 minutes. 3. Add chili powder, cayenne, cumin, tomatoes, tomato paste, green chilies, black beans, and stock, stir them well and stop the process. 4. Close the lid, turn the pressure release valve to SEAL position, and then move the slider to PRESSURE. Select HI and set the cooking time to 20 minutes. Press START/STOP to begin cooking. When finished, release the pressure naturally. 5. Serve the dish with sour cream, if desired.

**Per Serving:** Calories 362; Fat: 21.7g; Sodium: 1193mg; Carbs: 15.29g; Fibre: 9.2g; Sugar: 3.43g; Protein: 32.17g

## Cola Pulled Beef

**Prep Time:** 15 minutes | **Cook Time:** 80 minutes | **Serves:** 6

2 small yellow onions, halved and thinly sliced into half-moons
2 large garlic cloves, peeled
240 ml plain cola (do not use a diet soda)
60 g Worcestershire sauce
2 tablespoons apple cider vinegar
2 tablespoons ketchup-like chili sauce, such as Heinz
1 tablespoon mild paprika
1 teaspoon ground dried mustard
1 teaspoon table salt
½ teaspoon ground cloves
1 (1.3 kg) boneless beef chuck roast, cut into two chunks and any large bits of fat removed

1. Mix the onion, garlic, cola, Worcestershire sauce, vinegar, chili sauce, paprika, ground mustard, salt, and cloves in the pot. 2. Set the pieces of beef into this sauce, and then turn to coat on all sides. 3. Close the lid, turn the pressure release valve to SEAL position, and then move the slider to PRESSURE. Select HI and set the cooking time to 60 minutes. Press START/STOP to begin cooking. When finished, release the pressure naturally. 4. Use a meat fork and a large, slotted spoon to transfer the pieces of meat to a nearby cutting board. Use a flatware tablespoon to skim any excess surface fat off the sauce in the pot. Also find and discard the garlic cloves. 5. Bring the sauce to a simmer at Lo3 on SEAR/SAUTÉ mode, stirring quite often. Simmer until thickened like a wet, loose barbecue sauce, stirring almost all the while, 5 to 10 minutes. Meanwhile, shred the beef with two forks. 6. Once the sauce has reached the right consistency, stir the shredded meat into it and cook, stirring often, until well coated and most of the liquid has been absorbed, about 1 minute. 7. Stop the process, and set the lid askew over the insert, and set aside for 5 minutes to blend the flavors and let the meat absorb more sauce.
**Per Serving:** Calories 242; Fat: 10.23g; Sodium: 678mg; Carbs: 8.52g; Fibre: 1.2g; Sugar: 4.81g; Protein: 29.18g

## Beef Meatloaf

**Prep Time:** 20 minutes | **Cook Time:** 35 minutes | **Serves:** 4-6

900 g beef mince
80 ml milk
55 g panko breadcrumbs
1 yellow onion, grated
2 eggs, beaten
Salt and ground black pepper to taste
480 ml water
60 g ketchup

1. In a large bowl, combine the milk with breadcrumbs. Stir well and set aside for 4 to 6 minutes. 2. Then add whisked eggs, onion, salt and pepper to taste. Mix them well. 3. Add the beef mince to the bowl and stir well. 4. Add water to the pot and placing the rack in it. Place the meatloaf onto a sheet of nonstick aluminum foil and shape a loaf. Spread the ketchup on the top. 5. Place the meatloaf "boat" on the rack. 6. Close the lid, turn the pressure release valve to SEAL position, and then move the slider to PRESSURE. Select HI and set the cooking time to 35 minutes. Press START/STOP to begin cooking. When finished, release the pressure naturally. 7. Slice and serve with cooked potatoes or rice.
**Per Serving:** Calories 403; Fat: 20.58g; Sodium: 240mg; Carbs: 7.58g; Fibre: 0.5g; Sugar: 4.35g; Protein: 44.37g

## Caribbean Pulled Pork

**Prep Time:** 15 minutes | **Cook Time:** 1 hour 30 minutes | **Serves:** 8

360 ml water
100 g chopped dried pineapple
1 small red onion, chopped
One 100 g can mild or hot green chiles
1 tablespoon molasses
Up to 1 teaspoon hot red pepper sauce, such as Tabasco sauce
1 teaspoon dried thyme
1 teaspoon ground dried ginger
1 teaspoon ground allspice
½ teaspoon ground dried turmeric
½ teaspoon celery salt
½ teaspoon grated nutmeg
½ teaspoon table salt
1 (1.4 kg) bone-in pork shoulder or picnic ham, any skin and large blobs of fat removed

1. Stir the water, dried pineapple, onion, canned chilies, molasses, pepper sauce, thyme, ginger, allspice, turmeric, celery salt, nutmeg, and salt in the pot. Add the pork and turn to coat on all sides. 2. Close the lid, turn the pressure release valve to SEAL position, and then move the slider to PRESSURE. Select HI and set the cooking time to 90 minutes. Press START/STOP to begin cooking. When finished, release the pressure naturally. 3. Use a meat fork and a large, slotted spoon to transfer the pork (or pieces of it) to a nearby cutting board. Use a flatware tablespoon to skim any excess surface fat from the sauce. 4. Bring the sauce in the pot to a simmer at Lo3 on SEAR/SAUTÉ mode. Simmer until reduced to about 120 ml, stirring more and more frequently as it cooks, 7 to 10 minutes. 5. Meanwhile, shred the meat with two forks, discarding any additional blobs of fat. Stir the shredded meat into the sauce, and stop the process. 6. Serve warm.
**Per Serving:** Calories 381; Fat: 24.26g; Sodium: 2113mg; Carbs: 8.85g; Fibre: 0.7g; Sugar: 6.19g; Protein: 32.34g

## Rosemary Lamb Cubes

**Prep Time:** 25 minutes | **Cook Time:** 25 minutes | **Serves:** 6-8

1.8 kg. lamb, boneless and cut into 2.5 – 5 cm cubes
Salt and ground black pepper to taste
2 tbsp. olive oil
4 cloves garlic, minced
3 tbsp. flour
360 ml veggie stock
120 g carrots, sliced
4 rosemary sprigs

1. Season the lamb with salt and pepper to taste. 2. Select SEAR/SAUTÉ. Select Lo3, and then press START/STOP to begin cooking. 3. When hot, heat the oil and sauté the garlic for 1 minute; brown the lamb; stir in the flour and pour in the stock. 4. Add the carrots and rosemary, and stop the process. 5. Close the lid, turn the pressure release valve to SEAL position, and then move the slider to PRESSURE. Select HI and set the cooking time to 25 minutes. Press START/STOP to begin cooking. When finished, release the pressure naturally. 6. Remove the rosemary stems. 7. Serve the lamb with sauce.
**Per Serving:** Calories 656; Fat: 42.29g; Sodium: 411mg; Carbs: 8.23g; Fibre: 0.8g; Sugar: 1.08g; Protein: 57.24g

## Red Wine Braised Beef Brisket

**Prep Time:** 50 minutes | **Cook Time:** 20 minutes | **Serves:** 4-6

1.4 kg beef brisket, flat cut
3 tbsp. olive oil
1 tsp. salt
1 tsp. ground black pepper
1 large onion, sliced
1 carrot, chopped
1 stalk celery, diced
1 tbsp. tomato paste
2 cloves garlic, minced
240 ml beef stock
240 ml red wine
2 sprigs fresh thyme
1 bay leaf

1. Rub all sides of the beef brisket with salt and pepper. 2. Select SEAR/SAUTÉ. Select Lo3, and then press START/STOP to begin cooking. 3. When hot, heat 2 tablespoons of oil, and brown the beef for 4 to 5 minutes on each side. Transfer the meat to a plate. 4. Pour in 1 tablespoon of oil and add onion, carrot, celery, and tomato paste. Sauté them for 4 to5 minutes; add the garlic and cook for another 30 to 45 seconds. 5. Pour in the stock and red wine and deglaze the pot by scraping the bottom to remove all of the brown bits. 6. Return the meat to the pot and add thyme and bay leaf, and then stop the process. 7. Close the lid, turn the pressure release valve to SEAL position, and then move the slider to PRESSURE. Select HI and set the cooking time to 60 minutes. Press START/STOP to begin cooking. When finished, release the pressure naturally. 8. Transfer the brisket to a serving plate and slice the meat. Press the SAUTE key and simmer until the sauce thickens. 9. Serve the brisket with sauce.
**Per Serving:** Calories 550; Fat: 42.28g; Sodium: 3265mg; Carbs: 6.11g; Fibre: 1.2g; Sugar: 2.75g; Protein: 34.58g

## Palatable Pork Tenderloin

**Prep Time:** 20 minutes | **Cook Time:** 26 minutes | **Serves:** 4-6

900 g pork loin
½ tsp. sea salt or to taste
½ tsp. ground black pepper
1 tbsp. dry onion, minced
2 tbsp. extra virgin olive oil
1 yellow onion, chopped
2 apples, chopped
480 ml apple cider
2 tbsp. brown sugar

1. Rub all sides of the pork loin with salt, pepper and dried onion. 2. Select SEAR/SAUTÉ. Select Lo3, and then press START/STOP to begin cooking. 3. When hot, heat the oil and brown the meat for 4 minutes on each side. Remove the pork loin from the pot. 4. Add the onion and sauté for 2 minutes. Add the apples and apple cider and deglaze the pot by scraping the bottom to remove all of the brown bits. 5. Return the pork to the pot and sprinkle with sugar. Stop the process. 6. Close the lid, turn the pressure release valve to SEAL position, and then move the slider to PRESSURE. Select HI and set the cooking time to 20 minutes. Press START/STOP to begin cooking. When finished, release the pressure naturally. 7. Slice the pork loin and serve with the remaining sauce.
**Per Serving:** Calories 416; Fat: 20.46g; Sodium: 320mg; Carbs: 17.71g; Fibre: 2.7g; Sugar: 13.59g; Protein: 39.22g

## Beef Short Ribs with Carrots

**Prep Time:** 20 minutes | **Cook Time:** 46 minutes | **Serves:** 6-8

1.7 kg beef short ribs
1 tsp. salt
1 tsp. ground black pepper
2 tbsp. olive oil
3 cloves garlic, minced

4-6 carrots, cut into bite sized pieces
240 g onions, diced
1 tbsp. dried thyme
360 ml beef stock

1. Rinse and pat the ribs dry with paper towels. 2. Season the ribs with salt and pepper. 3. Select SEAR/SAUTÉ. Select Lo3, and then press START/STOP to begin cooking. 4. When hot, heat the oil, and then brown the ribs for 5 minutes on each side. Transfer the browned ribs to a plate. 5. Add the garlic to the pot and cook for 1 minute; add carrot, onion and thyme, and sauté them for another 5 minutes until softened. 6. Add the stock and deglaze the pot by scraping the bottom to remove all of the brown bits. 7. Put the beef ribs back into the pot, and stop the process. 8. Close the lid, turn the pressure release valve to SEAL position, and then move the slider to PRESSURE. Select HI and set the cooking time to 35 minutes. Press START/STOP to begin cooking. When finished, release the pressure naturally. 9. Serve the dish with cooked rice, potato or veggies.

**Per Serving:** Calories 436; Fat: 23.91g; Sodium: 580mg; Carbs: 9.61g; Fibre: 1.6g; Sugar: 2.22g; Protein: 46.61g

## Honey Pork Chops

**Prep Time:** 25 minutes | **Cook Time:** 10 minutes | **Serves:** 4

900 g pork chops, boneless
½ tsp. sea salt or to taste
¼ tsp. ground black pepper
1 tbsp. olive oil
2 tbsp. Dijon mustard
½ tbsp. maple syrup

70 g honey
2 tbsp. water
2 cloves garlic, ground
½ tsp. cinnamon
½ tsp. fresh ginger, peeled and minced

1. Rub all sides of the pork chops with salt and pepper. 2. Combine the Dijon mustard, maple syrup, honey, water, garlic and cinnamon in a bowl. 3. Select SEAR/SAUTÉ. Select Lo3, and then press START/STOP to begin cooking. 4. When hot, heat the oil and brown the meat for 3 to 4 minutes per side. Pour the mixture into the pot. 5. Stop the process. 6. Close the lid, turn the pressure release valve to SEAL position, and then move the slider to PRESSURE. Select HI and set the cooking time to 15 minutes. Press START/STOP to begin cooking. When finished, release the pressure naturally. 7. Serve the dish with mashed potatoes and macaroni and cheese as sides.

**Per Serving:** Calories 584; Fat: 28.74g; Sodium: 503mg; Carbs: 20.67g; Fibre: 0.6g; Sugar: 19.16g; Protein: 58.61g

## Mushroom Lamb Ragout

**Prep Time:** 25 minutes | **Cook Time:** 70 minutes | **Serves:** 4-6

675 g lamb, bone-in
1 tsp. vegetable oil
4 tomatoes, chopped
2 tbsp. tomato paste
225 g mushrooms, sliced
6 cloves garlic, minced
1 small yellow onion, chopped
2 carrots, sliced
1 tsp. oregano, dried
Water as needed
Salt and ground black pepper to taste
A handful parsley, finely chopped

1. Select SEAR/SAUTÉ. Select Lo3, and then press START/STOP to begin cooking. 2. When hot, heat the oil and sear the lamb for 4 minutes on each side until nicely browned; add tomatoes, tomato paste, mushrooms, garlic, onion, carrots, oregano and water to cover everything, and then stir in the salt and pepper. Stop the process. 3. Close the lid, turn the pressure release valve to SEAL position, and then move the slider to PRESSURE. Select HI and set the cooking time to 60 minutes. Press START/STOP to begin cooking. 4. When finished, release the pressure naturally. 5. Transfer the lamb to a plate, then discard bones and shred the meat. 6. Return the shredded lamb to the pot, add the parsley and stir. 7. Serve warm.
**Per Serving:** Calories 441; Fat: 20.44g; Sodium: 101mg; Carbs: 35.69g; Fibre: 6g; Sugar: 4.6g; Protein: 32.87g

## Potato Lamb Stew

**Prep Time:** 20 minutes | **Cook Time:** 30 minutes | **Serves:** 4

675 g lamb stew meat, cut into 4 cm cubes
2 tbsp. olive oil
3 tbsp. soy sauce
3 cloves garlic, chopped
1 big white onion, chopped
400 g sweet potatoes, chopped
**Spices:**
½ tsp. allspice
½ tsp. ground turmeric
1 tsp. ground cumin
½ tsp. ground ginger

360 g carrots, chopped
2 cans tomatoes, diced
120 g kale, finely chopped (stems removed)
5 dried unsweetened apricots, finely chopped
840 ml chicken or beef stock

½ tsp. curry powder
1 tsp. cinnamon
1 tsp. salt
½ tsp. ground black pepper

1. Select SEAR/SAUTÉ. Select Lo3, and then press START/STOP to begin cooking. 2. When hot, heat the oil and cook the lamb cubes until browned. 3. Add the remaining ingredients and spices to the pot and stop the process. 4. Close the lid, turn the pressure release valve to SEAL position, and then move the slider to PRESSURE. Select HI and set the cooking time to 30 minutes. Press START/STOP to begin cooking. When finished, release the pressure naturally. 5. Serve warm.
**Per Serving:** Calories 502; Fat: 14.89g; Sodium: 1626mg; Carbs: 59.77g; Fibre: 11.1g; Sugar: 26.38g; Protein: 35.71g

# Chapter 7 Desserts

## Cranberry Stuffed Apples

**Prep Time:** 10 minutes | **Cook Time:** 5 minutes | **Serves:** 5

5 medium apples
85 g fresh or frozen cranberries, thawed and chopped
55 g packed brown sugar
2 tbsp. chopped walnuts
¼ tsp. ground cinnamon
⅛ tsp. ground nutmeg
Optional toppings: Whipped cream or vanilla ice cream

1. Core apples, leaving bottoms intact. Peel top third of each apple. 2. Add 240 ml water to the pot and place in the rack. 3. Combine the cranberries, brown sugar, walnuts, cinnamon and nutmeg; spoon into apples. Place apples on rack. 4. Close the lid, turn the pressure release valve to SEAL position, and then move the slider to PRESSURE. Select HI and set the cooking time to 3 minutes. Press START/STOP to begin cooking. When finished, release the pressure naturally. 5. Serve the dish with whipped cream or ice cream if desired.

**Per Serving:** Calories 195; Fat: 2.18g; Sodium: 6mg; Carbs: 46.2g; Fibre: 4.7g; Sugar: 37.75g; Protein: 1.26g

## Arroz Leche

**Prep Time:** 10 minutes | **Cook Time:** 20 minutes | **Serves:** 6

200 g long-grain white rice, rinsed until the water runs clear
480 ml milk
300 ml water
2 tablespoons granulated sugar
⅛ teaspoon fine sea salt
1 (250 g) can sweetened condensed milk
1 teaspoon vanilla extract

1. Combine the rice, milk, water, sugar, and salt in the pot. 2. Close the lid, turn the pressure release valve to SEAL position, and then move the slider to PRESSURE. Select HI and set the cooking time to 20 minutes. Press START/STOP to begin cooking. When finished, release the pressure naturally. 3. Stir in the sweetened condensed milk and vanilla. 4. Serve the dish warm or let cool to room temperature.

**Per Serving:** Calories 206; Fat: 4.53g; Sodium: 111mg; Carbs: 33.72g; Fibre: 0.4g; Sugar: 9.41g; Protein: 6.36g

## Tart Apple Comfort

**Prep Time:** 30 minutes | **Cook Time:** 15 minutes | **Serves:** 8

| | |
|---|---|
| 240 ml water | 240 g heavy whipping cream |
| 6 medium tart apples, peeled and sliced | 1 tsp. vanilla extract |
| 200 g sugar | 40 g digestive biscuit crumbs |
| 30 g plain flour | 60 g chopped pecans |
| 2 tsp. ground cinnamon | 55 g butter, melted |
| 2 large eggs | Vanilla ice cream, optional |

1. Add 240 ml water to the pot. 2. In a large bowl, combine apples, sugar, flour and cinnamon. Spoon the mixture into a suitable baking dish. 3. In a small bowl, whisk eggs, cream and vanilla; pour over apple mixture. 4. In another bowl, combine cracker crumbs, pecans and butter; sprinkle over top. 5. Loosely cover dish with foil to prevent moisture from getting into dish. Place the dish on a rack with handles; lower into pressure cooker. 6. Close the lid, turn the pressure release valve to SEAL position, and then move the slider to PRESSURE. Select HI and set the cooking time to 12 minutes. Press START/STOP to begin cooking. When finished, release the pressure naturally. 7. Serve the dish warm, with ice cream if desired.

**Per Serving:** Calories 304; Fat: 17.37g; Sodium: 64mg; Carbs: 37.79g; Fibre: 4.4g; Sugar: 27.66g; Protein: 2.52g

## Oats Stuffed Apples

**Prep Time:** 10 minutes | **Cook Time:** 5 minutes | **Serves:** 4

| | |
|---|---|
| 120 ml fresh orange juice | 20 g quick-cooking oats |
| ½ teaspoon orange zest | ½ teaspoon ground cinnamon |
| 55 g packed light brown sugar | 4 cooking apples |
| 30 g golden raisins | 4 tablespoons butter, divided |
| 30 g chopped pecans | 240 ml water |

1. In a small bowl, mix together orange juice, orange zest, brown sugar, raisins, pecans, oats, and cinnamon. Set aside. 2. Rinse and dry the apples. Cut off the top fourth of each apple. Peel the cut portion of the apple. Dice it and then stir into the oat mixture. Hollow out and core the apples by cutting to, but not through, the apple bottoms. 3. Place each apple on a piece of aluminum foil that is large enough to wrap the apple completely. 4. Fill the apple centre s with the oat mixture. Top each with 1 tablespoon butter. 5. Wrap the foil around each apple, folding the foil over at the top and then pinching it firmly together. 6. Pour the water into the pot and place in the rack. Place the apple packets on the rack. 7. Close the lid, turn the pressure release valve to SEAL position, and then move the slider to PRESSURE. Select HI and set the cooking time to 5 minutes. Press START/STOP to begin cooking. When finished, release the pressure naturally. 8. Carefully unwrap apples and transfer to serving plates. Enjoy.

**Per Serving:** Calories 300; Fat: 17.22g; Sodium: 101mg; Carbs: 39g; Fibre: 5.6g; Sugar: 28.15g; Protein: 2.25g

## Flan in Jar

**Prep Time:** 25 minutes | **Cook Time:** 10 minutes | **Serves:** 6

100 g sugar
1 tbsp. plus 240 ml hot water
240 ml coconut milk or whole milk
80 ml whole milk
80 ml sweetened condensed milk

2 large eggs plus 1 large egg yolk, lightly beaten
Dash salt
1 tsp. vanilla extract
1 tsp. dark rum, optional\

1. In a small heavy saucepan, spread sugar; cook, without stirring, over medium-low heat until it begins to melt. Gently drag melted sugar to centre of pan so sugar melts evenly. 2. Cook them for 2 minutes until melted sugar turns a deep amber color. Immediately remove from heat and carefully stir in 1 tbsp. hot water. Quickly pour into six hot 100 g. jars. 3. In a small saucepan, heat coconut milk and whole milk until bubbles form around sides of pan; remove from heat. 4. In a large bowl, whisk condensed milk, eggs, egg yolk and salt until blended but not foamy. Slowly stir in hot milk; stir in vanilla and rum (optional). 5. Strain through a fine sieve. Pour egg mixture into prepared jars. Centre lids on jars; screw on bands until fingertip tight. 6. Add remaining hot water to the pot and place rack insert in the bottom. Place jars on rack, offset-stacking as needed. 7. Close the lid, turn the pressure release valve to SEAL position, and then move the slider to PRESSURE. Select HI and set the cooking time to 6 minutes. Press START/STOP to begin cooking. When finished, release the pressure naturally. 8. Cool jars 30 minutes at room temperature. Refrigerate until cold, about 1 hour. Run a knife around the sides of the jars; invert flans onto dessert plates.

**Per Serving:** Calories 110; Fat: 3.61g; Sodium: 59mg; Carbs: 16.23g; Fibre: 0g; Sugar: 15.89g; Protein: 2.93g

## Typical Bread Pudding

**Prep Time:** 5 minutes | **Cook Time:** 25 minutes | **Serves:** 8

480 ml milk
5 large eggs
75 g granulated sugar
1 teaspoon vanilla extract

½ loaf cubed bread (5 cm cubes)
Nonstick cooking spray
2 tablespoons unsalted butter, cut into small pieces

1. In a medium bowl, combine the milk, eggs, sugar, and vanilla and stir until the sugar dissolves. Add the bread cubes and stir to coat well. Refrigerate them for 1 hour. 2. Grease the pot with nonstick cooking spray. Pour in the bread mixture. Scatter the butter pieces on top. 3. Close the lid, turn the pressure release valve to SEAL position, and then move the slider to PRESSURE. Select HI and set the cooking time to 25 minutes. Press START/STOP to begin cooking. When finished, release the pressure naturally. 4. Allow the pudding to cool for a few minutes before serving.

**Per Serving:** Calories 165; Fat: 7.5g; Sodium: 140mg; Carbs: 18.3g; Fibre: 0.6g; Sugar: 8.48g; Protein: 5.66g

## Easy Black & Blue Cobbler

**Prep Time:** 15 minutes | **Cook Time:** 15 minutes | **Serves:** 6

| | |
|---|---|
| 420 ml water, divided | 2 large eggs, lightly beaten |
| 120 g plain flour | 2 tbsp. whole milk |
| 300 g sugar, divided | 2 tbsp. rapeseed oil |
| 1 tsp. baking powder | 240 g fresh or frozen blackberries |
| ¼ tsp. salt | 240 g fresh or frozen blueberries |
| ¼ tsp. ground cinnamon | 1 tsp. grated orange zest |
| ¼ tsp. ground nutmeg | Whipped cream or vanilla ice cream, optional |

1. Add 240 ml of water to the pot. 2. In a large bowl, combine the flour, 150 g sugar, baking powder, salt, cinnamon and nutmeg. 3. Combine the eggs, milk and oil; stir into dry ingredients just until moistened. Spread the batter evenly onto the bottom of a greased baking dish. 4. In a large saucepan, combine the berries, remaining water, orange zest and remaining sugar; bring to a boil. Remove from the heat; immediately pour over batter. 5. Place a piece of aluminum foil loosely on top to prevent moisture from getting into dish; place on a rack with handles; lower into pressure cooker. 6. Close the lid, turn the pressure release valve to SEAL position, and then move the slider to PRESSURE. Select HI and set the cooking time to 15 minutes. Press START/STOP to begin cooking. When finished, release the pressure naturally. 7. Uncover the lid and let the food stand for 30 minutes before serving. 8. Serve the dish with whipped cream or ice cream if desired.
**Per Serving:** Calories 343; Fat: 7.01g; Sodium: 107mg; Carbs: 67.96g; Fibre: 4.9g; Sugar: 46.39g; Protein: 4.54g

## Vanilla Chocolate Custard

**Prep Time:** 15 minutes | **Cook Time:** 20 minutes | **Serves:** 4

| | |
|---|---|
| 4 large egg yolks | 360 ml milk |
| 2 tablespoons sugar | 110 g semisweet chocolate chips |
| Pinch of salt | 480 ml water |
| ¼ teaspoon vanilla extract | |

1. In a small bowl, whisk together egg yolks, sugar, salt, and vanilla. Set aside. 2. In saucepan over medium-low heat, heat milk to a low simmer. 3. Whisk a spoonful into the egg mixture to temper the eggs, and then slowly add the egg mixture back into the saucepan with remaining milk. 4. Add chocolate chips and continually stir on simmer for 10 minutes until chocolate is melted. Remove from heat and evenly distribute chocolate mixture among four custard ramekins. 5. Pour the water into the pot and place in the rack. Place ramekins on the rack. 6. Close the lid, turn the pressure release valve to SEAL position, and then move the slider to PRESSURE. Select HI and set the cooking time to 6 minutes. Press START/STOP to begin cooking. When finished, release the pressure naturally. 7. Transfer custards to a plate and refrigerate covered for 2 hours. Serve.
**Per Serving:** Calories 278; Fat: 15.46g; Sodium: 101mg; Carbs: 33.2g; Fibre: 1.9g; Sugar: 26.08g; Protein: 6.32g

## Poached Pears

**Prep Time:** 20 minutes | **Cook Time:** 5 minutes | **Serves:** 8

480 ml water
1 can pear nectar
240 ml tequila
100 g sugar
2 tbsp. lime juice
2 tsp. grated lime zest
1 cinnamon stick (8 cm.)
¼ tsp. ground nutmeg
8 whole Anjou pears, peeled
Sweetened whipped cream, optional
Fresh mint leaves

1. Select SEAR/SAUTÉ. Select Lo3, and then press START/STOP to begin cooking. 2. When hot, add the water, pear nectar, tequila, sugar, lime juice, lime zest, cinnamon, and nutmeg to the pot, and cook them for 3 minutes until sugar is dissolves. 3. Stop the process and add the pears to the pot. 4. Close the lid, turn the pressure release valve to SEAL position, and then move the slider to PRESSURE. Select HI and set the cooking time to 3 minutes. Press START/STOP to begin cooking. When finished, release the pressure naturally. 5. Reserve 720 ml cooking juices; discard remaining juices and cinnamon stick. Return the reserved juices to the pot. 6. Simmer the food at Lo2 on SEAR/SAUTÉ mode for 30 minutes until liquid is reduced to 240 ml. 7. Halve pears lengthwise and core. Serve with the sauce, whipped cream if desired, and mint leaves.

**Per Serving:** Calories 162; Fat: 0.25g; Sodium: 195mg; Carbs: 39.47g; Fibre: 5g; Sugar: 29.25g; Protein: 0.59g

## Cinnamon Bananas Foster

**Prep Time:** 10 minutes | **Cook Time:** 5 minutes | **Serves:** 4

8 tablespoons salted butter, cubed
60 ml light (clear) rum
60 ml water
205 g dark-brown sugar, packed
1 teaspoon cinnamon
1 teaspoon vanilla extract
6 good-sized bananas, firm but not green, peeled and sliced into 2.5 cm pieces
Vanilla ice cream, for serving

1. Combine the butter, rum, water, brown sugar, cinnamon, and vanilla in the pot until the large lumps of the sugar are dissolved and the mixture is the texture of molasses. The butter should remain chunky. 2. Add the bananas and stir gently to coat with the sauce. 3. Close the lid, turn the pressure release valve to SEAL position, and then move the slider to PRESSURE. Select HI and set the cooking time to 2 minutes. Press START/STOP to begin cooking. When finished, release the pressure naturally. 4. Let cool for a few moments before serving over bowls of vanilla ice cream.

**Per Serving:** Calories 541; Fat: 16.47g; Sodium: 168mg; Carbs: 102.43g; Fibre: 4.9g; Sugar: 78.66g; Protein: 3g

## Classic Lava Cake

**Prep Time:** 15 minutes | **Cook Time:** 20 minutes | **Serves:** 8

125 g plain flour
205 g packed brown sugar, divided
5 tbsp. baking cocoa, divided
2 tsp. baking powder
¼ tsp. salt
120 ml fat-free milk

2 tbsp. rapeseed oil
½ tsp. vanilla extract
⅛ tsp. ground cinnamon
300 ml hot water
Optional toppings: Fresh raspberries and ice cream

1. In a large bowl, whisk the flour, 105 g brown sugar, 3 tbsp. cocoa, baking powder and salt. In another bowl, whisk milk, oil and vanilla until blended. Add to flour mixture; stir just until moistened. 2. Spread the mixture into a baking dish coated with cooking spray. 3. In a small bowl, mix cinnamon and remaining brown sugar and 2 tbsp. cocoa; stir in hot water. Pour over batter but do not stir. 4. Add 240 ml water to the pot and place the rack in the pot. Cover the baking dish with foil. 5. Fold a piece of foil lengthwise into thirds, making a sling. Use the sling to lower the dish onto the rack. 6. Close the lid, turn the pressure release valve to SEAL position, and then move the slider to PRESSURE. Select HI and set the cooking time to 20 minutes. Press START/STOP to begin cooking. When finished, release the pressure naturally. 7. Carefully remove baking dish. Let stand 15 minutes. A toothpick inserted in cake portion should come out clean.

**Per Serving:** Calories 150; Fat: 4.12g; Sodium: 83mg; Carbs: 27.17g; Fibre: 1.4g; Sugar: 13.11g; Protein: 2.75g

## Walnut Chocolate Brownies

**Prep Time:** 20 minutes | **Cook Time:** 35 minutes | **Serves:** 10-12

6 tbsp. unsalted butter
4 tbsp. unsweetened cocoa powder
90 g plain flour
¾ tbsp. baking powder
200 g sugar

¼ tsp. salt
2 large eggs, beaten
30 g chopped walnuts
480 ml water

1. Preheat a small pan on the stove, add and melt the butter. 2. Remove from the stove and add the cocoa powder, mix well. 3. In a bowl, combine the flour, baking powder, sugar and salt. 4. Add the eggs and walnuts, stir. Add the cocoa mix and stir them well. 5. Grease a baking pan and add the batter. Cover the pan tightly with aluminum foil. 6. Pour the water into the pot and set the rack in the pot. Put the pan on the rack. 7. Close the lid, turn the pressure release valve to SEAL position, and then move the slider to PRESSURE. Select HI and set the cooking time to 35 minutes. Press START/STOP to begin cooking. When finished, release the pressure naturally. 8. Allow the brownies cool and serve.

**Per Serving:** Calories 121; Fat: 6.01g; Sodium: 55mg; Carbs: 16.1g; Fibre: 0.9g; Sugar: 8.26g; Protein: 2.07g

## Peaches with Cinnamon Whipped Cream

**Prep Time:** 15 minutes | **Cook Time:** 10 minutes | **Serves:** 6

- 360 g whipping cream
- 2 tablespoons powdered sugar
- 1 teaspoon ground cinnamon
- ½ teaspoon vanilla extract
- 2 cans sliced peaches in syrup
- 60 ml water
- 2 tablespoons packed light brown sugar
- 1 tablespoon white wine vinegar
- ⅛ teaspoon ground allspice
- 1 teaspoon ground ginger
- 1 cinnamon stick
- 4 whole cloves
- Pinch of cayenne pepper
- 3 whole black peppercorns

1. Pour whipping cream into a metal bowl. Whisk until soft peaks form. Slowly add powdered sugar, cinnamon, and vanilla and continue whipping until firm. Set aside and refrigerate. 2. Add remaining ingredients to pot. Stir them to mix. 3. Close the lid, turn the pressure release valve to SEAL position, and then move the slider to PRESSURE. Select HI and set the cooking time to 3 minutes. Press START/STOP to begin cooking. When finished, release the pressure naturally. 4. Remove and discard the cinnamon stick, cloves, and peppercorns. 5. Simmer the food at Lo2 on SEAR/ SAUTÉ mode for 5 minutes to thicken the syrup. 6. Serve the dish warm or chilled, topped with cinnamon whipped cream.

**Per Serving:** Calories 496; Fat: 11.37g; Sodium: 41mg; Carbs: 101.64g; Fibre: 1.9g; Sugar: 95g; Protein: 1.47g

## Brownie Cake

**Prep Time:** 10 minutes | **Cook Time:** 20 minutes | **Serves:** 6

- 4 tablespoons butter, room temperature
- 2 large eggs
- 40 g plain flour
- ½ teaspoon baking powder
- 15 g unsweetened cocoa powder
- Pinch of sea salt
- 75 g sugar
- 45 g semisweet chocolate chips
- 40 g chopped pecans
- 240 ml water
- 2 tablespoons powdered sugar

1. In a large bowl, whisk together butter, eggs, flour, baking powder, cocoa powder, salt, and sugar. Do not overmix. 2. Fold in chocolate chips and pecans. Pour batter into a greased 6" cake pan. Cover pan with a piece of aluminum foil. 3. Pour water into the pot and place in the rack, and then place the cake pan on the rack. 4. Close the lid, turn the pressure release valve to SEAL position, and then move the slider to PRESSURE. Select HI and set the cooking time to 20 minutes. Press START/STOP to begin cooking. When finished, release the pressure naturally. 5. Remove cake pan from the pot and transfer to a rack to cool. Sprinkle with powdered sugar and serve.

**Per Serving:** Calories 237; Fat: 16.65g; Sodium: 67mg; Carbs: 23.4g; Fibre: 2.7g; Sugar: 13.53g; Protein: 3.45g

## Pearberry Crisp with Topping

**Prep Time:** 15 minutes | **Cook Time:** 10 minutes | **Serves:** 4

**Pearberry Filling**
6 medium pears, peeled, cored, and diced
135 g thawed frozen mixed berries
60 ml water
1 tablespoon fresh lemon juice
2 tablespoons pure maple syrup
1 teaspoon ground cinnamon
¼ teaspoon ground nutmeg
Pinch of salt

**Topping:**
4 tablespoons melted butter
80 g old-fashioned oats
25 g plain flour
30 g chopped almonds
55 g packed light brown sugar
¼ teaspoon sea salt

1. Place all of the Pearberry Filling ingredients in the pot. Stir them to distribute ingredients. 2. Mix all of the Topping ingredients together in a small bowl. Spoon drops of topping over the filling. 3. Close the lid, turn the pressure release valve to SEAL position, and then move the slider to PRESSURE. Select HI and set the cooking time to 8 minutes. Press START/STOP to begin cooking. When finished, release the pressure naturally. 4. Spoon into bowls and enjoy.

**Per Serving:** Calories 343; Fat: 15.63g; Sodium: 271mg; Carbs: 56.06g; Fibre: 10.7g; Sugar: 28.37g; Protein: 7.06g

## Chocolate Custard

**Prep Time:** 30 minutes | **Cook Time:** 30 minutes | **Serves:** 4-6

240 g whole milk
240 g fresh cream
1 tsp. vanilla extract
100 g sugar
325 g. dark chocolate, chopped
6 whisked egg yolks
960 ml water

1. In a saucepan, combine and simmer the milk, cream, vanilla, and sugar, until sugar has dissolved. 2. Add the chocolate and remove the saucepan off the heat. 3. When the chocolate has melted, slowly stir in the whisked egg yolks. 4. Pour the mixture into a baking pan. 5. Add the water to the pot and placing the steam rack in it. Place the pan on the rack. 6. Close the lid, turn the pressure release valve to SEAL position, and then move the slider to PRESSURE. Select HI and set the cooking time to 30 minutes. Press START/STOP to begin cooking. When finished, release the pressure naturally. 7. Serve warm or chilled.

**Per Serving:** Calories 646; Fat: 44.8g; Sodium: 152mg; Carbs: 44.33g; Fibre: 6.7g; Sugar: 30.31g; Protein: 16.04g

## Flavorful Crème Brûlée

**Prep Time:** 10 minutes | **Cook Time:** 15 minutes | **Serves:** 4

480 g heavy cream
6 egg yolks
6 tablespoons granulated sugar
**The Crust:**
50 g granulated white or raw sugar (1 tablespoon per ramekin)
⅛ teaspoon nutmeg
⅛ teaspoon cinnamon
1½ teaspoons vanilla extract

1. Pour the cream into a microwave-safe bowl and microwave for 45 seconds. 2. Whisk the egg yolks, sugar, nutmeg, cinnamon, and vanilla into the warmed cream. 3. Divide the mixture into four 200 g ceramic ramekins and cover each with foil. 4. Place the rack in the pot with 480 ml of water. Rest the ramekins on top of the rack. 5. Close the lid, turn the pressure release valve to SEAL position, and then move the slider to PRESSURE. Select HI and set the cooking time to 15 minutes. Press START/STOP to begin cooking. When finished, release the pressure naturally. 6. Before removing the ramekins, allow them to cool for 5 minutes in the pot. 7. Remove the foil. The custard will appear a little jiggly, like Jell-O. Place the ramekins in the fridge for at least 4 hours, preferably overnight, until firm and like pudding in consistency. 8. When ready to serve, evenly sprinkle each ramekin with 1 tablespoon of sugar and very carefully, in circular motions, use a culinary torch or your grill to caramelise the top to the hue of your liking, and then serve.

**Per Serving:** Calories 369; Fat: 31.41g; Sodium: 36mg; Carbs: 16.44g; Fibre: 0.4g; Sugar: 15g; Protein: 5.64g

## Baked Honey Plums

**Prep Time:** 30 minutes | **Cook Time:** 15 minutes | **Serves:** 4-6

675 g fresh plums, pitted and halved
360 ml water
2 tbsp. honey
1 tsp. vanilla extract
4 cloves
1 star anise
3 cardamom pods
1 tsp. ground cinnamon

1. Put the plums into the pot. 2. Add the water, honey, vanilla, cloves, anise, cardamom, and cinnamon. 3. Close the lid, turn the pressure release valve to SEAL position, and then move the slider to PRESSURE. Select HI and set the cooking time to 15 minutes. Press START/STOP to begin cooking. When finished, release the pressure naturally. 4. Transfer the plums to a serving bowl. 5. Cook the food still in the pot at Lo4 on SEAR/ SAUTÉ mode until reduce the remaining liquid by half. 6. Serve or store the plums with the sauce.

**Per Serving:** Calories 128; Fat: 0.19g; Sodium: 23mg; Carbs: 33.24g; Fibre: 1.5g; Sugar: 31.15g; Protein: 0.55g

## Apple Cobbler

**Prep Time:** 10 minutes | **Cook Time:** 5 minutes | **Serves:** 4

5 Granny Smith apples, cored, peeled, and cut into 2.5 cm cubes, at room temperature
2 teaspoons ground cinnamon
½ teaspoon ground nutmeg
2 tablespoons maple syrup
2 tablespoons caramel syrup (plus more for topping at the end)

120 ml water
4 tablespoons salted butter
70 g light-brown sugar
60 g old-fashioned oats (not the instant kind)
30 g plain flour
½ teaspoon sea salt
Vanilla ice cream, for serving

1. Place the apples in the pot and top with the cinnamon, nutmeg, maple syrup, caramel syrup, and water. Stir them together well until a liquid consistency is reached and the apples are coated. 2. In a microwave-safe bowl, melt the butter, and then add the brown sugar, oats, flour, and salt. Mix them well and pour over the apple mixture in the pot. 3. Close the lid, turn the pressure release valve to SEAL position, and then move the slider to PRESSURE. Select HI and set the cooking time to 2 minutes. Press START/STOP to begin cooking. When finished, release the pressure naturally. 4. Serve right out of the pot, topped with vanilla ice cream and some more caramel sauce, if desired.

**Per Serving:** Calories 364; Fat: 10.43g; Sodium: 395mg; Carbs: 70.53g; Fibre: 9.5g; Sugar: 38.32g; Protein: 5.9g

## Lemon Mango Cake

**Prep Time:** 25 minutes | **Cook Time:** 35 minutes | **Serves:** 6-8

240 ml water
100 g sugar
180 ml milk
60 g coconut oil
1 tsp. mango syrup

155 g flour
¼ tsp. baking soda
1 tsp. baking powder
⅛ tsp. salt
1 tbsp. lemon juice

1. Pour the water into the pot and set a steam rack in the pot. 2. Grease a baking pan. Add the sugar, milk, and oil to the pan and stir until sugar melts. 3. Add the mango syrup and stir. Add the flour, baking soda, baking powder, and salt. Stir them to combine. 4. Add the lemon juice and stir them. 5. Place the pan on the rack. 6. Close the lid, turn the pressure release valve to SEAL position, and then move the slider to PRESSURE. Select HI and set the cooking time to 35 minutes. Press START/STOP to begin cooking. When finished, release the pressure naturally. 7. Let the cake cool for 10 minutes and serve.

**Per Serving:** Calories 171; Fat: 7.76g; Sodium: 91mg; Carbs: 23.05g; Fibre: 0.5g; Sugar: 8.05g; Protein: 2.75g

## Pumpkin-Spice Brown Rice Pudding

**Prep Time:** 60 minutes | **Cook Time:** 10 minutes | **Serves:** 6

200 g brown rice
120 ml water
720 ml almond milk
90 g dates, pitted and chopped
A pinch of salt

1 stick cinnamon
200 g pumpkin puree
1 tsp. pumpkin spice
140 g maple syrup
1 tsp. vanilla extract

1. Pour the boiling water over rice and wait for 10 minutes. Rinse the rice. 2. Add the water and milk to the pot. 3. Boil the liquid at Lo4 on SEAR/SAUTÉ mode, and then add the rice, dates, salt, and cinnamon to the pot. 4. Close the lid, turn the pressure release valve to SEAL position, and then move the slider to PRESSURE. Select HI and set the cooking time to 10 minutes. Press START/STOP to begin cooking. When finished, release the pressure naturally. 5. Add the pumpkin puree, pumpkin spice, and maple syrup to the pot, and stir them well. 6. Cook the mixture at Lo4 on SEAR/SAUTÉ mode until thickened. 7. Stop the process, remove the cinnamon stick and stir in the vanilla. 8. Transfer the pudding to a serving bowl and let it cool for 30 minutes. Serve.

**Per Serving:** Calories 495; Fat: 12.48g; Sodium: 186mg; Carbs: 84.03g; Fibre: 9.6g; Sugar: 30.24g; Protein: 14.28g

## Butter Banana Cake

**Prep Time:** 35 minutes | **Cook Time:** 35 minutes | **Serves:** 6-8

110 g butter, soft
200 g sugar
3 medium eggs, beaten
1 tsp. baking powder
1 tsp. cinnamon

1 tsp. nutmeg
¼ tsp. salt
250 g plain flour
3 bananas, peeled and mashed
240 ml water

1. In a bowl, whisk together butter, sugar, and eggs until combined. 2. Add the bananas, cinnamon, nutmeg, and salt. Mix them well. Stir in the flour and baking powder. 3. Grease a baking pan with butter. Pour the batter in the pan and cover with foil. 4. Pour the water into the pot and set the rack in the pot. Place the baking pan on the rack. 5. Close the lid, turn the pressure release valve to SEAL position, and then move the slider to PRESSURE. Select HI and set the cooking time to 50 minutes. Press START/STOP to begin cooking. When finished, release the pressure naturally. 6. Let the cake cool for a few minutes and serve.

**Per Serving:** Calories 391; Fat: 13.58g; Sodium: 189mg; Carbs: 62.76g; Fibre: 2.2g; Sugar: 33.31g; Protein: 5.93g

# Conclusion

A feature-rich kitchen gadget, the Ninja Foodi Max Multi Cooker may be used for air frying, steaming, pressure cooking, and more. The Ninja Foodi Max Multi-excellent cooker's cooking features and enormous capacity to feed the entire family make it quick and simple to prepare delectable dinners, sides, snacks, and desserts. An entire chicken may fit in and be cooked in the fryer basket, which has a good capacity. Utilize pressure cooking to cook delicate meals up to 70% quicker than conventional methods, followed by crisping to give your food a beautiful golden finish.

# Appendix Recipes Index

## A
Almond Cranberry Quinoa 22
Apple Cobbler  98
Arroz Leche  89

## B
Bacon & Veggie–Packed Frittatas  20
Baked Honey Plums  97
Barbecue Pulled Pork Sandwiches  80
Barbecue Tofu Sandwiches  38
Beef Bow-Ties in Spicy Tomato-Almond Sauce  83
Beef Enchiladas  81
Beef Meatloaf  84
Beef mince Stew 36
Beef Reuben Soup  33
Beef Short Ribs with Carrots  87
Beer-nana Loaf  21
Broccoli with Garlic Dressing  38
Brown Butter Pasta with Scallops & Tomatoes  73
Brownie Cake  95
Butter Banana Cake  99

## C
Cannellini Beans with Tomatoes  41
Caramelised Vegetable Strata  26
Caribbean Pulled Pork  85
Carrot Chicken Tikka Masala  59
Carrot Lamb Ragù  79
Celery Tuna Noodle Casserole  70
Cheese Broccoli Risotto  46
Cheese Macaroni Soup  33
Cheese Ravioli Casserole  47
Cheese Sandwiches  76
Cheese Squash Soup  32
Chicken Lettuce Wraps  52
Chicken Sausage Gumbo  52
Chicken Sausage Ragu  51
Chicken Scarpariello  62
Chickpeas with Spinach  49
Chili Onion Mac 28
Chili Texas  31
Chili without Bean  29

Chipotle Salmon  66
Chocolate Custard  96
Cinnamon Bananas Foster 93
Classic Lava Cake  94
Cocktail Prawns  67
Coconut Prawns  66
Cola Pulled Beef 84
Crab Legs with Lemon Wedges  74
Cranberry Stuffed Apples  89
Crescent Rolls  22
Crispy Parmesan Polenta  40
Crustless Mini Quiche Bites  25
Crustless Vegetable Potpie 50
Curried Chickpeas with Coriander  44

## D
Duck Chunks with Potato Cubes  54

## E
Easy Black & Blue Cobbler  92
Easy Breads  23
Egg White Bites  24
Enchilada & Sweet Potato Casserole  47
Enchilada Casserole  23
Enchilada Chicken Soup  34

## F
Feta Beef with Olives  79
Flamboyant Flamenco Salad  39
Flan in Jar  91
Flavorful Crème Brûlée  97

## G
Garlic-Chili Fish Tacos  71
Garlic-Lemon Turkey Breast  54
Glazed Whole Turkey  63
Gravy Pork Chops with Onion  77
Gruyère Crustless Quiche  25

## H
Healthy Black Bean Soup 30
Herbed Pork Loin  76
Herb-Loaded Warm Potato Salad  48
Honey "Baked" Cauliflower  46
Honey Pork Chops  87

Honey-Garlic Salmon 71

**I**

Italian Roast Ragù 82

**J**

Japanese-Style Vegetable Curry 40

**K**

Ketchup Chicken Wings 63

**L**

Lamb Mince with Black Beans 83
Lamb Stew in Beef Stock 36
Lemon Mango Cake 98
Lemon-Seasoned Quinoa 19
Lentils & Bulgur 45
Loaded Bacon Potato Soup 37

**M**

Mexican Beef Casserole 78
Middle Eastern Lentils & Rice 39
Millet Porridge 18
Minestrone Soup 27
Mongolian Beef 75
Mozzarella Pork Chops 82
Mushroom & Chicken Chunk Stroganoff 56
Mushroom Chicken Soup 28
Mushroom Lamb Ragout 88

**O**

Oats Stuffed Apples 90
Old Bay-Seasoned Lobster Tails 72
Onion Chicken Shawarma 60
Onion Prawns Gumbo 65
Orange Chicken Thighs & Vegetables 58

**P**

Palatable Pork Tenderloin 86
Peaches with Cinnamon Whipped Cream 95
Pearberry Crisp with Topping 96
Pecan Bacon Strips 45
Pesto Chicken Pieces with Quinoa 53
Pesto Tilapia with Sun-Dried Tomatoes 72
Poached Pears 93
Pork Ragù 77
Pork Stew with Tomatoes & Pinto Bean 30
Potato Lamb Stew 88
Pumpkin-Spice Brown Rice Pudding 99

**Q**

Quick Prawns Boil 70

**R**

Red Curry Prawns 67
Red Lentil and Bulgur Soup 43
Red Wine Braised Beef Brisket 86
Rosemary Lamb Cubes 85
Round Roast with Veggies 78

**S**

Salmon with Zesty Dill Sauce 74
Sausage & Bean Soup 32
Sausage Quinoa 21
Savory Turkey Wings 64
Scallop Risotto with Spinach 73
Simple Firehouse Chili 37
Soy Salmon with Broccoli 69
Spanish Tortilla with Sauce 18
Spiced Kidney Bean Stew 42
Spicy Chicken 35
Spinach Eggs Florentine 19
Stew Beef and Broccoli 80
Stuffed Poblano Peppers 49
Stuffed Potato Soup 29
Sweet Potato & Wild Rice Chowder 27

**T**

Tangy Thai Bash Orange Chicken 55
Tart Apple Comfort 90
Thai Curry Salmon 68
Tikka Chicken Masala 57
Tomato Tortellini 48
Turkey Breast Casserole 56
Turkey Breast Roast in Chicken Stock 59
Turkey Breast with Vegetables 61
Turkey Salsa Verde 55
Typical Bread Pudding 91

**V**

Vanilla Chocolate Custard 92
Vanilla Quinoa 20
Vegetables & Chicken Breasts 35
Veggie & Duck Chunks 61
Veggie Chicken Casserole 53

**W**

Walnut Chocolate Brownies 94

Printed in Great Britain
by Amazon